LEADERSHIP
FROM WITHIN

LEADERSHIP
FROM WITHIN

Peter Urs Bender
with Eric Hellman

Published in 1997 by
Stoddart Publishing Co. Limited
34 Lesmill Road,
Toronto, Canada
M3B 2T6

Distributed in Canada by
General Distribution Services Limited
34 Lesmill Road,
Toronto, Canada M3B 2T6
Tel. (416) 445-3333
Fax (416) 445-5967
E-mail Customer.Service@ccmailgw.genpub.com

01 00 99 98 97 1 2 3 4 5

Cataloguing in Publication Data
Bender, Peter Urs, 1944–
Leadership from within

ISBN 0-7737-5903-4

1. Leadership.   II. Title.

HD57.7.B45 1997   658.4'092   97-931931-5

Cover design: Pekoe Jones
Text design: Tannice Goddard

Printed and bound in Canada

Leadership from Within™ is a trademark of Peter Urs Bender.

MISSION STATEMENT

To analyze, understand, and explain
the elements of leadership
in the most practical way

and

To inspire leadership qualities
in all Canadians

Contents

Acknowledgements

I never expected I would do another book.

Secrets of Power Presentations, my first (and I thought my only) book, was a great success. To date, over 100,000 have been printed. It is now on reading lists in over forty Canadian universities and colleges. It has also been published in Indonesian, French, German, and Russian.

So why this one?

I have been teaching "Leadership from Within" in seminars, keynotes, and speeches since 1994. They have been very successful and numerous audiences have asked me when it would be in book form. I always thought "*never*" – but I kept that to myself.

Then, in October 1996, I had lunch with Eric Hellman. Eric had been writing articles in my name for about a year. He had also attended some of my seminars, transcribed my audiotapes, and revised my last book; he basically knows my work better than anyone. Even more important than knowing my message, he knows my philosophy.

At the time, Eric mentioned that business was not too rosy for him.

He was considering taking on a part-time job to keep his cashflow going. So I made him an offer: To write this book, based on my seminar and keynotes, my philosophy and life experience. If not for him, this would not have happened. I just did not have the time.

There are many others to whom I also owe a lot of gratitude. John Robert Colombo, author/creator of over one hundred books and general editor of the *The Canadian Global Almanac*, was extremely helpful. He gave ideas for my survey of Canadian high achievers and contributed several stories on leadership. George Torok, my first Power Presentations seminar licensee, gave me many suggestions and wonderful quotes, which you will find inside.

Don Bastian and the staff of Stoddart Publishing have been excellent to work with. Marnie Kramarich in particular did a marvellous (and thorough!) editing job. Thanks to the marketing and media work of Jeannine Rosenberg and Patti McCabe, I believe *Leadership from Within* will be another Canadian success.

Last but not least, I would like to thank my wife Frances – for allowing me to invest so much of my time and my life in my work. I know it is not easy to live with someone like me . . .

A Special Note of Thanks

In preparing for this book, I surveyed a number of Canadian high achievers. I wanted to learn their thoughts and advice on how to become a leader. I want to thank each and every one of them for their important contributions to this book, and for helping to improve the quality of Canadian life through their work and achievements. In particular, my thanks to Seymour Schulich for encouraging me to outperform myself.

Finally, to my readers . . .

Thank you for reading *Secrets of Power Presentations* and this book. Without you, I would not have a reason to speak or to write. Your ideas help me, your support encourages me, and your results inspire me.

If you read *Secrets of Power Presentations*, I believe you will love this book. You already know how to give a great presentation. *Leadership from Within* will help get the best of you into your speeches — and your life!

It's Up to You

If you want a quick fix, don't bother to go through my book. I don't believe in taking bubble baths to increase self-esteem. It helps to be clean, but self-esteem and leadership come from a way of thinking and living. There are no shortcuts to a more fulfilled life.

Enjoy my book and remember:

> *One sees what one wants to see;*
> *One hears what one wants to hear;*
> *One reads what one wants to read.*

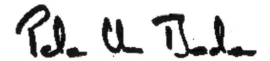

Preface

Over the years, I have developed two main themes for the keynotes, seminars, and workshops I give to organizations. One deals with the skills of making "power presentations." The other focuses on developing the qualities of leadership that I call "Leadership from Within."

While I had not thought about it consciously, the two always seemed connected. I have only recently begun to see why.

Leadership + Presentation Skills = Success

To make powerful presentations, you must be "connected" with your message. You have to know it inside out; feel it; live it; and express it with passion. The more intimately you know your topic and the more you believe in and want to share it with others, the more powerful you will be in presenting it. *The same is true for leadership*.

The most powerful leader is the one who leads "from within." Not by a set of texts or what they learned in business school. Those help. But the power that comes from purpose and experience, and the leadership that comes from vision, are qualities that reside within us.

Powerful leadership comes from knowing yourself. Power presentations come from expressing yourself effectively.

In *Secrets of Power Presentations*, I outlined the quintessentials of speaking and presenting. This book is about knowing *what* to communicate — by developing the leadership qualities you have inside.

I hope you find it useful and effective. Please let me know what you think, and how I can make it even better.

Survey of Canadian Leaders

One of the best ways to become a leader is to study what other leaders have done — and then do it yourself. So, for this book, I decided to ask some of Canada's high achievers to share their ideas on what makes a leader. They contributed their favourite sayings and tips; stories of their experiences; and how they would rate some key ingredients for success.

Their ideas are sprinkled throughout the book. For a full list of respondents, and a summary of factors they believe are important for leadership, see the Appendix.

WHAT IS LEADERSHIP FROM WITHIN?

THE SEARCH FOR LEADERS

Leadership is like beauty —
it's hard to define but
you know it when you see it.
— WARREN BENNIS

In these rapidly changing times, we are faced with many challenges. Making ends meet and climbing out of debt. Finding a new job after a "downsizing." Succeeding in business despite global competition. Raising well-adjusted children. Resolving painful conflicts in our relationships. Coping with illness and the loss of loved ones. To say nothing of facing the many social and world problems we see in the media daily.

Scared about the future, with our attitudes becoming tougher, more hostile and cynical, we look for someone or something to turn to.

We need leadership. Yet few of us have much confidence in our traditional leaders — in government, religion, or business. Why are we so short on good leaders? Where are we going to find them?

After years of studying people — in my work as a professional speaker, and in teaching, management, and sales — I have come to three basic conclusions.

First, I believe that leadership starts from within. We all possess the seeds of greatness. In this respect, we are no different from Winston

Churchill, Golda Meir, General George Patton, or Mahatma Gandhi.

Second, I have found that there are skills we can learn to develop these "seeds." It is the degree to which we do so that determines our success.

Third, I am convinced that the biggest thing that blocks us is *fear*. Most of us are afraid to stand out. To say what we feel. To risk being criticized or looking foolish. It is this fear that stops us from being the leaders we are looking for in the world.

This book is about giving you the skills to be your own leader.

WHO IS A LEADER?

A leader* is someone who:

- guides someone or something on a way, especially by going on in advance
- directs on a course or in a direction
- directs the operations, activities, or performance of others
- goes at the head of (e.g., a parade)
- is first among many.

*Adapted from the *Merriam Webster Collegiate Dictionary*

Leaders are found in every field of human endeavour. Every industry, government, and community; every group, company, or association. Just think about the people you and others respect the most.

Maybe it's a top salesperson or senior executive in your company. A national politician or the person across the street who runs a Neighbourhood Watch program. Perhaps it is one of your parents, for the way they raised you.

Take time to look for leaders. Ask others who it is they respect. The more you look, the more you will find them. And just by watching what they do, you will become more like them.

Towards a New Definition of Leadership

Leadership is the art of getting people to do what
they don't want to do and have them enjoy the experience.
— Major-General (retired) Lewis MacKenzie, MSC, CD
UN Commander, Peacekeeping Forces, Sarajevo

Leadership consists of the capacity to get people to do what
one wants them to do, or to chart a course, or to inspire.
— Laurier L. LaPierre, OC
Canadian author and broadcaster

Everyone has a different perspective on what leadership is.

I believe the best leaders demonstrate five key attributes. They:

- Raise awareness
- Show direction
- Create results
- Demonstrate to others how to reach a goal
- Achieve progress that benefits others, not just themselves.

Many people see leadership as "leading someone else." However, I believe it begins with leading *ourselves*.

Defined in this way, leadership is first and foremost an "inside job." We have to be able to lead ourselves before we can lead others. Like an inventor, we must have both the vision of a new product *and* the ability to create it. Like an explorer, we need to know there is a "new land" *and* show others how to get there. Like a coach, we have to identify talents in people around us *and* work with them to create outstanding results for the team. Or, like a top quality manager, we have to draw on the best within us before we can do so with our people.

This inner leadership, what I call "leadership from within," is very different from telling others what to do or the "do as I say, not as I do" approach that many of us have been taught.

Everyone thinks of changing the world,
but no one thinks of changing himself.
— LEO TOLSTOY

There are also some who see leadership as finding ways to get *tasks* accomplished more effectively. Re-engineering of systems. Quality control to reduce defects. Downsizing to increase financial returns. These are part of the process, but not the most important.

To me, leadership is about creating a better, stronger you. If I help you develop the qualities of a leader, you can apply these new skills to any task — selling, engineering, communicating — and accomplish it more effectively. If your self-esteem is better, you will do whatever you do better. If you carry an attitude of excellence, your goal will be to do your best. This is what I look for in the people I work with, and the companies I buy my products and services from. It is also what I want for my clients and the readers of this book.

Task-oriented people do not see things the same way leaders do. They may be and often are very good at what they do, but they do not yet see the big picture, which includes:

- how important each person is to the success of the group
- the perspective of their employers, co-workers, clients, or customers
- a long-term vision that motivates them to move forward
- their own value or how their part contributes to the whole.

Therefore they are not as fulfilled.

Two men were laying bricks in a field on the edge of town. A stranger walked up to one and asked, "What are you doing, friend?" The worker rather grumbled his answer. "I'm laying bricks," he said, and with that went on with his job.

Still wondering what they were doing, the stranger approached the second man. "So you're laying bricks, are you?" he asked. The worker looked up, somewhat surprised. "Not me," he said with a smile, eyes turning towards the sky. "I am building a cathedral."

My former home, Switzerland, is a very task-oriented country. The Swiss are industrious and excellent craftspeople. But they are not very happy. They have a very rich society, but *they do not see it.*

In some ways, they are similar to Canadians. The whole world speaks very highly about Canada. It is often voted the number one country to live in. Yet we Canadians often fail to see what we have. We focus on what is wrong or what is missing. As a result, we are becoming more pessimistic and cynical, and our commitment to keeping Canada together is declining.

Leadership is changing

In the past, leading meant being out in front. Ranking first in sales. Having the highest position. Scoring the most goals or getting the most votes. But leadership is changing. As we enter the 21st century, we need to see it in a new way. Here are some of the signs of the "new leadership."

1. *Leadership is about people.*
   Leadership is not just about managing systems, sales, equipment, and numbers. It's about people. The other things are tools and measures to help us make progress. Therefore, we need to change our bottom line to address: Am I more fulfilled? Are people stronger and happier? Is life getting better? We also need ways to measure our success in reaching these goals. Measures like profit and Gross Domestic Product are not enough.

   Statistics don't bleed. People do.
   – AUTHOR UNKNOWN

   A business that makes nothing but money is a poor kind of business.
   – HENRY FORD

2. *Leadership is about being the leader of you.*
   Find your own vision, put it into action, and you will automatically become the leader of others.

It's your life. Do not live to someone else's standard. Live to your own.

3. *Leadership is about internal motivation.*
   When many of us think of leadership, we see a rock-jawed, hard-nosed army officer yelling at his troops: "Shape up or get the hell out!" Many leaders of companies treat their employees the same way. This is understandable, since the design of organizations comes from the military model. It even still works in certain industries and countries.

   However, I believe this old form of leadership is quickly becoming outdated. We are moving from a "command and control" approach to one that "coaches and empowers." Sooner or later, people begin to resent and resist external control. When they do, work satisfaction and productivity decline.

4. *Leadership is about striving for perfection, while accepting our imperfections.*
   You and I not are not perfect. We want to accomplish goals and reach our visions. But often we do not. We fail. At these times, being a leader means accepting that we are human.

   A survey of the top one hundred companies that were (at the time) run by their original founders reported that these entrepreneurs had failed an average of *seven* times before succeeding. The list included people like Walt Disney and Ray Kroc, the founder of McDonald's.

   There is nothing wrong with failure –
   if you get back up again.

5. *Leadership is about change.*
   The world we live in brings thousands of challenges. Financial. Emotional. Physical. Many bring pain and frustration. You can go through them kicking and cursing, wishing things would stay the same. Holding on to what you have. Or you can make a decision to change.

We all have faults and self-defeating habits. The mistake is not in having them. The mistake is choosing not to change them.

Leadership is about making conscious choices to bring about positive change.

- Look clearly at your life right now. Is it what you want it to be? Are you happy with it? Did you accomplish enough? How are the people around you?
- What do you want to experience? Would you be prepared to try something new to have it?
- Consider changing what is not working. Are you willing?

Don't change because this or any other book tells you to. Forget the "guilt trip." Change because it is something you want to do.

6. *Leadership is about having confidence.*
   To consciously choose to change, you need to believe that things can get better. Yet we are in uncertain times – and we will be in uncertain times for many years to come. Confidence is lacking. Many are afraid to take leadership, to express their views, or to be different. Work on building your confidence.

7. *Leadership is about growth.*
   All progress is about going beyond what we have done before. There is a "leader" in a baby starting to walk. A teenager going on his first date. A recent graduate starting her first job. A couple getting engaged and married (or even divorced!). There is leadership in every invention or discovery ever made. If you are growing, you are a leader.

8. *Leadership is about having energy.*
   Most leaders have a great deal of energy. Your energy level comes from your thoughts and feelings. If you expect something good to happen or believe in a positive future, you will have a higher energy level.

Think of it this way. You arrive home exhausted after a long week of work. You have absolutely no energy. Then you get a call from a close friend you have not seen in years. You suddenly spring to life. Where did the *energy* come from?

How do you create positive energy around you? Try smiling! People around you will smile back. (They may think you are crazy. But I guarantee you they will smile.) They will start to feel and work better. You will feel happier and more energized.

Remember: *Energy is contagious.* The way you treat your employees is the way they will treat their customers and co-workers. That is how the spirit of an organization grows – either positively or negatively.

This is true for any relationship. For parents and children. Teachers and students. Husbands and wives. The public and politicians. (Think about it.)

9. *Leadership is about creating a positive experience.*
    We want to feel good about ourselves. We want to feel in control, powerful, and excited about what lies ahead.

    Remember the feeling of having a new love in your life? Or starting a new job? You had excitement, passion, and joy. It didn't last. But it felt great for a while.

    This may sound crazy . . . but now is the time to make your life feel that way again. Make changes at work. At home. With friends. Make it humorous. Alive. Spontaneous. Do things that motivate you to do more. After all, you can choose to be bored – or you can choose to live.

> *Change all projects to increase their excitement,*
> *urgency, and transformative potential.*
> *Sell the most exciting and provocative*
> *projects you can create.*
> — TOM PETERS

10. *Leadership is about creating results – with integrity.*
    Many people talk about what they would like to see happen. Politicians speak about reducing deficits, making our communities healthier or safer, and creating jobs. Business leaders speak of improving company profits or employee morale. Everyone talks about winning the lottery . . .

    Vision *is* important. But it's not enough. True leadership is the ability to turn vision into results: Getting out of debt. Creating more jobs and happier employees. Starting that new business. Going on the trip you have always wanted. Saying what you want to do, and doing it.

    But I am going to give you one caution. Whatever "it" is, do *not* do it at any cost. Do it so you "win" and others do, too. Do it with caring and respect. Do it with integrity. Fulfillment comes from having both your needs and your values satisfied. One without the other will leave you feeling incomplete.

11. *Leadership is about reducing fear and increasing hope.*
    In times of change, people are uncertain about their future. With this comes fear – of losing their jobs, economic security, company or social benefits, status, friendships, and other aspects of life they have come to value and depend upon. This fear saps motivation, reduces trust, and increases resistance.

    If you need to lead people through significant change, even times of hardship, find a way to increase their hope. Inspire and demonstrate that you care about them. Improve the tangible bottom line *and* people's sense of confidence. How you implement change is as important as the results you create.

Qualities and ingredients of leadership

On the next page are some words and phrases I have come to associate with leadership over the years – with additions from the leaders I surveyed for this book. As you review the list, place a checkmark beside those you consider most important.

Ingredients of Leadership

___ Know yourself/values

___ Vision

___ Passion

___ Risk-taking

___ Communication skills

___ Checking progress/results

___ Hard work

___ Persistence

___ Goal-setting

___ Associate with the right people

___ Knowledge of your field

___ Belief in yourself

___ Desire to succeed

___ Doing what you love

___ Loving what you do

___ Positive attitude

___ Good with people

___ Trust instincts/gut feel

___ Do as you promise

___ Confidence

___ Courage

___ Honest and trustworthy

___ Focused

___ Take initiative and responsibility

___ Motivate/inspire others

___ Caring/compassionate

___ Give credit, acknowledge excellence

___ Endurance/stamina

___ Thorough/handle details

___ Able to work under pressure

Some people excel in one particular area. Others have strength in many. Remember: You do not have to be Number One to be successful at life. It is the total package that makes you a winner.

> *To be judged as honest and trustworthy*
> *by both allies and adversaries.*
> – INGREDIENT FOR SUCCESS RECOMMENDED
> BY DENNIS MCDERMOTT, FORMER PRESIDENT,
> CANADIAN LABOUR CONGRESS

WHAT ARE THE GOALS OF LEADERSHIP?

1. Leaders seek fulfillment

As I've said, many see leading as having the most of something, like sales, money, or power. Yet we have all heard about the wealthy person who is unhappy or has no friends. The powerful person who wins without integrity or honesty. Or the top sports figure who abuses himself or others. They may be "stars." But they do not seem like leaders. Why is that?

Money, fame, and power are highly desirable signs of progress. But they are actually stepping stones to a larger goal. How much you enjoy being who you are. How satisfied you are with what you have. How much love and friendship you have. How secure you are within.

It is not how many toys you get,
it is how much satisfaction you get from your toys.

I believe the ultimate goal of leadership is personal and shared fulfillment. You may find this in becoming top in your field. Building a successful company. Helping those less fortunate. Or improving the environment. But those are simply accomplishments. Your happiness is the true measure of your success.

I am not saying that getting the basics – food, money, housing, sales, profits, good grades – are not important. They are! I have just found that these come more easily when we are more fulfilled.

Studies have found that confident people perform better and are more successful. Relaxed people are able to think more clearly and act more effectively in tough situations. The ones who smile get paid more and are given more responsibility. Those with self-esteem are more likely to raise others to have self-esteem. They are all connected.

II. Leaders make progress

The second reason to become a leader is to *lead yourself from where you are now to where you want to be.* Leadership is about learning what will bring you joy, peace, and fulfillment, and doing it. Not in isolation from others, but in collaboration *with* them.

True leaders think for themselves. They take responsibility. They have more internal motivation to start new projects, and the persistence to accomplish them. Leaders develop a wider range of skills and the ability to handle many tasks.

Good leaders know that all our interests are connected. They listen well. They see what others need. They support people in accomplishing their objectives. And because they give of themselves, they receive in return.

By developing these qualities, you will be more valuable to organizations. You will be happier with yourself. Other people will want you around. And whether you are working for yourself or others, you will be more successful.

How Do We Make Progress?

If leadership is about making progress, how do we get where we want to go? Think of it like making a trip.

		Where you
You are here		want to go

How you are going to get there

"You Are Here"

Every journey starts with where you are right now – and that is the result of what you have done, up until now, with what you have been given.

Life is not fair. None of us has had a perfect past. You may have had bad cards dealt to you: bad parents, bad genes, or bad relationships. You may have suffered from hardships, a sick body, or discrimination. But you have a choice. Are you going to blame the problem for keeping you where you are now? Or are you going to use it to move ahead?

It may be hard to accept, but the past was "perfect" to get you where you are now. Where you will be in another few years depends on what you do between now and then.

"Where Are You Going?"

Do you like where you are? Do you want to continue in the same direction or grow in a different direction? This is an opportunity to make a choice, and to move in the direction you want to take.

If you don't know where you are going,
any road will get you there.
— ANONYMOUS

Having a goal is essential for getting you where you want to go. It focuses your energy and guides your decisions. It helps you use your resources and talents effectively to reach your destination. Knowing where you are going also helps determine how you will get there.

If you are in Toronto and you want to get to Vancouver, you don't fly east (unless you have an around-the-world ticket, of course).

If you want to become a millionaire by the age of forty, you can't spend all your time working as a counterperson at McDonald's.

If you want be fulfilled at your work, you can't spend your whole life hating your job.

These choices simply will not help you achieve your objectives. Similarly, complaining about what is wrong does not make things better.

You have to make some decisions – about where you want to go; what you want to do; and what you want to experience!

"How Will You Get There?"
Michelangelo had a vision of what he wanted to create, and used his artistic skills to paint the Sistine Chapel.

Eleanor Roosevelt cared about people and wanted a more humane world. She used her speaking and people skills to help create the United Nations Declaration of Human Rights.

Your mother had (many) ideas of what she wanted to cook, and used her cooking skills to make you great dinners. (That may have been a few years ago, but I am sure you still remember!)

Having decided on your "destination" or what you want to accomplish, you then have to take action to get there.

III. Leaders create results

Attitudes and *behaviour* are the "vehicles" that get us where we want to go, the "tools" we use to create our *results*. This is true for everyone – engineers and artists; CEOs and secretaries; teachers and students; even saints and sinners!

Attitudes + Behaviour ➡ Results

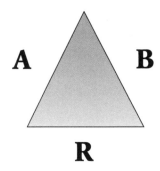

A   B

R

Attitude is the way you think and feel. It is based on the choices you've made about how best to cope and live in this world. Attitudes can be positive or negative, ranging from:

"Life is a bitch"	to	"Life is a beach"
"There is nothing I can do – I have no power"	to	"The world is full of opportunity"
"I hate what I do"	to	"I love what I do"
"What I do is not important"	to	"My life makes a difference."

Behaviour is what you do to express these attitudes in your life.

If Attitude + Behaviour is negative, the results will be negative. The reverse is also true. When you make your attitude and behaviour more positive, your results improve. The evidence is all around us: in our jobs, relationships, communities, and in ourselves.

It used to be that when things went wrong, we blamed people's *behaviour*. "He does not act properly." "She should have better manners." Today, we focus more on *attitude*. "They just don't care." "She does not take responsibility." "He has an attitude problem." *Both* are important.

While you can often pressure others into changing their behaviour, it is harder to change their attitudes. Just think of when people have tried to change yours!

In fact, it is actually impossible to change people's attitudes. You can only influence them. Pressure or guilt may create short-term change. But for the long term, you must help others create a different picture inside. This applies to your children, your employees, or anyone you want to lead. Help them see where they want to go or how they want to feel. Then show them which attitudes and behaviour will be most successful in getting them the results they seek.

> *The greatest discovery of this generation:*
> *Human beings can alter their lives*
> *by altering their attitudes.*
> — WILLIAM JAMES

Do you remember being told when you were a kid to "change your attitude"? I never knew what that meant. Behaviour you can change. But attitudes — your thoughts and feelings — are harder to change. It is like changing your identity, your way of seeing life.

That's true. In fact, seeing life differently or "changing perspective" is one of the keys to changing your attitude.

If you haven't already, start practising how to shift perspective. Try finding opportunities in the midst of problems. Look at what people are doing right instead of what they are doing wrong. Sometimes it is not easy, but there are benefits. Your feelings will shift. You will become more hopeful. You will see new ways of doing things, and eventually you will get better results.

"Results" Have Two Parts

When someone wins at the Olympics or achieves any outstanding goal, they get two rewards. One is the tangible prize – for example, the medal – plus all the praise and attention they receive. The other is a more positive self-image, and the great feeling that goes with winning.

All accomplishments have these two parts: a tangible, physical part and an intangible, thought-feeling part. Looked at in another way, it is partly outer, the behaviour; and partly inner, the attitude. Remember this the next time you are working to improve your results or those of someone else. You cannot improve the outer bottom line unless you improve the inner bottom line as well.

Many companies have found that productivity improvement mechanisms – such as re-engineering, new technology, loss reduction, TQM (Total Quality Management), goal-setting, management by objective – do not have a lasting impact. That is what happens if you just change people's behaviour. You may get them acting differently. But if you leave their minds and hearts behind, you've made a big mistake.

> *Help other people get what they want –*
> *and you'll get what you want.*
> – MARY KAY ASH

WHAT TYPE OF LEADER ARE YOU?

We are all leading all the time. By our words and by our example. At work. At home. In relationships. We even lead when we are by ourselves because leadership is not just a role; it is a way of thinking, a way of being, a way of life.

An important part of leadership is knowing what leads *you*. For example, do you have a strong sense of values? Are you controlled by your emotions? Do you make all decisions rationally, without much feeling? Do you go along with what is popular or what others say?

I use two terms to describe the way people lead or are motivated. One I call the leader-from-without. The other I call the leader-from-within. It's important to realize that we all have both within us. What matters is which one we decide to follow.

The leader-from-without

The leader-from-without is driven by the "beggars, tyrants, and temptresses" of life. Fears, pressures, and desires. Fears of not having enough of something, whether that be income, respect, power, food, sex, whatever. Daily pressures, such as catering to demanding clients, fighting fires, and meeting deadlines. And negative desires that are "too great to resist," such as lying to get the sale; putting others down to improve our own self-image; or leaving our values behind in order to get ahead.

Leaders-from-without can be the heads of companies, departments, or projects. Yet they are actually "out of control," because they are being driven by these inner and outer forces.

They do not respect or value themselves. They want to be accepted and are afraid of being wrong. So instead of doing what they think is best, they do what others say. They base their actions on public or media opinion. The current rage of management thinking. The dictates of their bosses, spouses, or co-workers. Or even what their parents or teachers told them, many years ago.

When this "leader" is directing your life, you are more prone to stress, anger, and conflict. You feel as if someone else is controlling you or trying to take over. There are constant battles over who is right or wrong. You feel the need to defend what you say and do. With this also comes resistance to change, and mistrust of those who do or see things differently.

The leader-from-within

The leader-from-within is moved by a different power. An inner direction and purpose. A desire to help, foster, and grow. A sense of flow or a fire within. Yet this passion is not out of control and it does not seem to run out. In fact, it's just the opposite. It is focused and harnessed. It is a self-renewing and enthusiasm-creating power that comes from a well-spring within.

Put another way, it is the same kind of energy that makes a dog wag its tail or a cat purr. You just feel good inside about whatever it is you are doing.

The leader-from-within brings increased well-being — to you, your organization, and the whole. You will start to thrive on collaboration and synergy. You will begin to view impossibles as possibles; and competitors as cooperators, potential partners for new ventures that neither of you could have taken on alone.

This leader also creates results. As I said earlier, these seem to come more easily when you are more fulfilled from within. When you are more confident, relaxed, and focused, you perform better. You are able to think more clearly and be more effective under pressure. You smile more, have higher self-esteem, and actually *enjoy* working more.

Paradoxically, you may not need to work as much. You will put less pressure on yourself to perform to unreasonable standards. You will not feel the need to "keep up with the Joneses." And your self-worth will be based less on what you have, and more on how you feel.

Leadership from within is more effective because it is whole. It combines head *and* heart. Power and compassion. Toughness with gentleness. Commitment to succeed with forgiveness of failure. This wholeness is very important. Traditional leadership and success have been based on the "head *over* heart" approach. There has been no room for feelings. This has led us to win-lose competition, office politics, and a higher degree of stress for those who were "successful" under the old leadership. (It is a fact that more heart attacks occur before 9 a.m. on Monday morning than at any other time of the week!)

Values make the difference

In the midst of the pressures of everyday life, how does the leader-from-within stay in charge? I believe it starts with values.

Each of us needs something within to guide us; to give wisdom, hope, and courage when times get rough. This can come from religious beliefs, or from the ethics, morals, or values you were raised with.

Without values, the leader-from-without will take control. But with them, you will find the confidence and power to focus your life in a positive direction.

Values provide:
a foundation — for growth and developing wisdom
a touchstone — something to turn to and connect with
confidence — to know what is right
guidance — to know which way to turn
inner peace — a sense of safety and security
strength — anchors you can hang on to
certainty — in the midst of change
continuity — something that lasts.

Yet values are not static or unquestioned. They are continually being refined and renewed.

The Leader-from-Without	**The Leader-from-Within**
Says one thing, does another	Walks the talk
Leads through fear and control	Leads with trust and by example
Sees separate interests	Sees shared interests
Tries to hold on to power	Shares power; empowers others
Wants things done his/her way	Encourages personal initiative
Tells others what to do	Invites ideas and feedback
Sets unrealistic deadlines	Sets reasonable deadlines
Is externally motivated	Is internally motivated
— by money, power, fame	— by values and principles
Is driven by fear and pressure	Seeks satisfaction, well-being
Disregards/puts down feelings	Sees caring/feelings as essential

HOW TO BECOME A LEADER-FROM-WITHIN

Despite the advantages of following the inner leader, we consistently choose the leader-from-without. There are three key reasons why this is so: fear, habit, and education.

If you look at the above lists, you will see that the two "leaders" are essentially opposites of each other. It takes a big leap in attitude and behaviour to shift from one to the other. This new way is quite foreign to our old way of thinking, and we become afraid.

Most of us were educated in the leadership-from-without school of life. We were raised to believe that it's a dog-eat-dog world and that we should always "look out for number one." In business, we learned the art of win-lose relationships and were told to leave our emotions at home. We learned not to speak up. Not to follow our dreams. Not to take risks.

Shifting to the leader-from-within requires confidence and strength, which will come through practice, encouragement, and positive reinforcement. These in turn will come as you read and apply the ideas in this book.

You must also recognize that the people around you may *not* support you in this: not because you are wrong, but because they (and the leader-from-without in you) are used to the old ways. So do not expect your current friends and associates to be immediately positive.

To balance this, look for those who are walking the same road and who understand what it takes to have vision and live with passion. Seek out the ones who stand out from the crowd and take risks. It may seem lonely at times. But you will find them.

Also be gentle with yourself when you start to worry or have doubts. Remember that with practice, you will strengthen your attitude muscles and see new behaviour. You will find others of like mind. They will give you encouragement and you will give it to them. The results you get will be the positive reinforcement you need to continue. Success may take a while. But you *can* do it — so stick with it!

It is not the IQ that counts.
It's the I CAN!

Do what you do so well that
when other people see what it is that you do,
they will want to see you do it again . . .
and they will bring others with them
to show them what it is that you do.
— WALT DISNEY

Five steps to leadership

I believe there are five key steps to developing "Leadership from Within."

1. Know Yourself
2. Have Vision and Passion
3. Take Risks
4. Communicate Effectively
5. Check Progress and Results

In the following chapters, I explore these in detail. But don't wait until you're finished the book to change your attitudes and behaviour:

Start now to

> Be a leader
> Feel like a leader
> Act like a leader
> Express like a leader
> Be seen as a leader
> Follow other leaders
> See and support the leader in others.

The rest will follow.

The Parade
When I was a little boy growing up in Switzerland, my grandmother told me a story. She said, "Urs [my Swiss name], there is a parade out there. Everyone plays a different role in it. Some people look at the parade. Some walk in it. And some lead the parade."

I ran excitedly to her window, hoping to catch a glimpse of the celebration outside. I lifted myself up on the window ledge to peer out. But to my dismay, I saw no parade. It left me wondering for many years what my grandmother was talking about.

In my seminars, I tell people the same story. "There is a parade going on out there. There are leaders, followers, and observers. Some people do not even know it is going on. That parade is your life. What role do you want to play?"

Maximize Your Return!

Genius is one percent inspiration,
and ninety-nine percent perspiration.
– THOMAS EDISON

I want you to get the utmost out of this book – and out of your life. So as you read through the chapters that follow, keep in mind the goals and qualities of true leaders. Invest yourself in discovering the leader-from-within in you. Find at least one thing you value in each chapter and apply it where you work. Then do whatever you can to create positive results. If you do, you will be more effective and fulfilled by the time you reach the final page.

Your journey to leadership will be easier if you understand the following four basic ideas, which I'll briefly describe below:

- How most people learn
- The relationship between effort and return
- How to set SMART goals
- The importance of support.

How Most People Learn

For me, learning is the key to life. It's what makes us grow. It's how we become successful — by finding out how life works, and then applying what we've learned to make our own lives work. That learning process usually involves the following steps:

1. *Intention and desire.*
   Learning begins with an intention — an interest in knowing more. It grows with willingness, and an openness to new ideas, perspectives, and skills. And it is fueled by desire. The more you want to learn, the more you will learn.

   I have often said, "If you're green, you grow. If you're ripe, you rot." Recognize that there is always more to learn. He who thinks he knows everything often knows nothing.

2. *Awareness.*
   Being "aware" is being conscious and awake. It is seeing what is around you. Hearing what people say and feel. Studying what makes things work. Awareness is both receptivity to the outside world, and sensitivity to your inner self.

   With awareness also comes a sense of direction. What do you want to learn? What do you need to learn? What do others need or want of you?

   Your direction is shaped by many factors. It is motivated by your ideals: it is based on your values; and it is guided by what is possible — both today and in the future.

3. *Information.*
   Awareness brings us many types of information. Facts and figures — to the left brain. Vision, sounds, and images — to the right brain. Feelings — to the heart. All of these "inform" us about our reality.

4. *Action.*
   If you want to learn, it's not enough just to read. You have to do. Apply. Implement. Act. This is what gives us experience. It

is the key to getting the most out of this book or any other.

5. *Results.*

When you learn you get three types of results.

First is the joy of learning. Most of us enjoy seeing things differently, gaining insight and understanding, and feeling we have grown.

The second result is discovering what we can do with our learning. It gives us more power to create and to fulfill our dreams and desires.

Third is our ability to share what we know. A great sense of satisfaction can come from teaching and helping others.

In this book, I have tried to give you all of these components of learning. Ideas to stimulate and inspire the leader in you. Information that describes how to be a leader. Actions you can take to become a stronger leader. And ways to improve the results you are getting.

Don't just accept what I say. As a matter of fact, you may disagree with certain statements I make. But that's okay . . . you have the right to be wrong!

When you find good ideas, test them. See what works. My goal is to give you the tools to be a leader in your life. But *you* have to use them.

A wise man can learn from a fool. But a fool never learns.
— ANONYMOUS

Exercise is a part of learning

A lot of people hate the idea of exercise. (So do I.) It implies having to do something you don't want to do — and forcing yourself to keep doing it. So take that idea and turn it around.

Exercise is a way to *develop a skill or ability that you* **want** *to have.* Say you want to be an entrepreneur. Then watching TV programs about successful business people is a form of exercise. (Try telling that to your spouse tonight!) If you want to improve your confidence, taking risks —

like speaking up at a meeting when you would normally stay silent – is also exercise. If you want to improve your energy or your thinking, going for a walk or a run will help you do it.

My focus in this book is on finding "exercises" that you are motivated to do because you can see the benefits.

At the end of each major section, I have given some exercises to help you strengthen your leadership muscles. They are designed to reinforce the inner you, so you will be a more powerful leader.

The exercises have three parts: Ask, Act, and Associate. By asking questions, you will increase self-awareness and learn from others. By taking action, your skills and experience will increase. By associating – or "hanging around" other leaders – you will get good ideas, feedback, knowledge, and support.

Remember: It is the *experience* resulting from *practice* that will help you feel better and reach your goals. Do whatever you can to build these exercises into your day. The more you invest, the more you will be paid back.

Spaced repetition

How well do you remember information? The date of your anniversary? Names of people you meet? Telephone numbers? What you had for lunch yesterday?

Most people don't remember very much about what they read or hear. That's why spaced repetition is so important. All it means is that if you do something more than once, you will remember more about it.

Here is how to apply it.

First, read this book through quickly. See if you agree with the main ideas and find them useful. Have a pen handy. Put a checkmark in the margin beside key points. Cross out what you disagree with. (As long as you don't cross out the whole book, it is okay with me.)

Then go through the book again. Take longer this time. Think about how you can apply it in your daily work. Highlight or underline key information. Use different colours. Make notes. In fact, make a mess out of it; not just because I may sell more that way, but because you will learn and remember more — and get the *utmost* from it!

The Relationship Between Effort and Return

Many of us start projects but do not complete them. We have great ideas but fail to reach our goals.

This is partly because we do not get results fast enough. We work hard for a time. But the effort we put in is greater than the results we get back, so we stop.

Success reinforces progress. It encourages us to keep going. Without it, our confidence begins to decline. We start to doubt ourselves, questioning the benefit of what we are doing. We think it will not work — and then we pull out before it does.

But look out! This is a trap! Why? Because of the principle of "Effort and Return." The following graph shows what I mean.

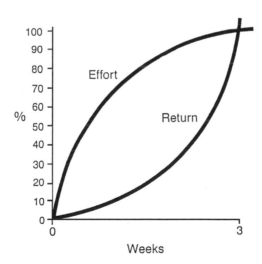

This graph represents the effort and return invested over time on a typical project. In the graph, you can see that the line for effort rises much more sharply than the line for return. Halfway into the project, over 80 percent of the effort has been invested – yet less than 20 percent of the return has been reaped. Towards the end of the project, effort declines as the return increases. So what does this mean?

With any new project, you need to build up "momentum." That is, you need to invest more at the beginning than you get out. The reward or the return comes later. I'm sorry to say that. But it's true.

Think about what it's like to learn a new musical instrument. You put in many hours of practice, and still you sound like the soundtrack of a horror movie. But at a certain point, it shifts. Beautiful melodies begin to come forth. It's the same way with singing. Learning a new language or beginning a new hobby. Learning a trade or starting a new business. (Boy, does it take time to get *that* started!)

In everything you undertake, you are making an investment. Initially, you will put in more time, energy, and maybe money than you get out. But if it is a sound project – and you stick with it – you will get a "return" on your investment. You may benefit financially; by gaining experience and contacts; or by learning life's lessons like patience and persistence. Not every project pays off in tangible ways. But if you give your best, you will reap many benefits.

This "investment attitude" will also help you to have patience. If you realize up front that it takes a while to get results, you can prepare yourself for the effort you have to put in. (It is like having a baby. No matter how much you may want it in five months, Mother Nature says, "Sorry. This one takes nine . . .")

Remember this on the road to being a leader. Be ready to invest in yourself. Do not expect rewards right away. But *know* that one way or another, you will be rewarded in the end.

There is no such thing as "all of a sudden."

Look at a company. Is it all of a sudden bankrupt? Not likely. Or how about a couple that all of a sudden gets a divorce? You can't tell me they didn't have problems beforehand. Then there's the star who became an "overnight success." Right. All of a sudden – after many years of hard work.

Most change begins a long time before it is noticed. Do not seek to be successful all of a sudden. Seek to be a success today, and every day. Work at it. Stay with it. Keep putting in the effort – and you will get your return.

How to Set SMART Goals

I am a strong believer in goals.

Too often in life, we get stuck in patterns that are not working. We do things that fill our days, but do not pay off in results. That is why it is important to have goals. They move us forward.

Simply defined, a goal is something you want to accomplish. It motivates you to reach for it. This can be something material, like having a new car or a bigger home. It could be creating your own business; developing new, lasting relationships; or giving yourself more time off work.

To achieve a goal, you must focus your attention and energy, and take action. Only by doing this will you see all that you can accomplish and get the good feelings that come with success.

To some, "having goals" means making a list each night of ten things they intend to do tomorrow. To others, it is deciding on something they want to do in the coming week. Still others see it as working towards a long-term vision. Everyone has some kind of goal – even if they do not consciously practise "goal-setting."

I want to share an idea that has worked for me. It is called the SMART formula. When I set a goal, I make sure it is:

S pecific   It should be clearly defined, not vague.
M easurable   It can be measured.
A ttainable   It is within my power to do.
R ealistic   It is possible and not just a pipedream.
T ruthful   It is something I really want to do.

Here's an example:

"I will complete project XYZ by the end of this week."

S: Completion of project XYZ is a specific goal (as opposed to a general statement like "I will do some more work on it").

M: Completion by the "end of the week" is measurable.

A: Is this something you can complete by yourself? If others are involved, it is probably not attainable by you alone.

R: Is it realistic to think you can complete the whole project by the end of the week? If not, pick a more manageable section of it, and do that.

T: Do you really want to do this project? If not, select something you *want* to accomplish.

This formula helps me in many ways. It is easy to remember. Because it reminds me to select realistic goals, I know I will actually do them. It also helps me set measurable goals – so I can check my progress along the way. I highly recommend it to you.

Having a clear vision is essential. If you *really* know what you want, you will probably get it. The vision will carry you through the tough times. If your vision is not strong, problems may stop your progress. (By the way . . . *everyone* experiences problems. High achievers and non-achievers. The high achievers have learned how to get past them.)

Persistence is another key. Major change usually does not happen overnight (or "all of a sudden"). But one step, each day, towards your goals will bring outstanding results. Stick with it.

Note: I want to make one thing very clear. I am not perfect – so I am not expecting you to be perfect, either! We all have up times and down times. One day you might feel like taking on the world. The next, you might feel down in the dumps.

In times like this, ease off the pressure. Get off your own back. Respect your feelings, and give your inner self some nurturing. When you're ready to get back into it, you'll feel stronger and rejuvenated – rather than drained or burnt out.

How you feel will determine
how you perform.

The Importance of Support

To accomplish anything in life, you will need to give and receive support. Support can come in many forms: Feedback. Caring. Financial assistance. Emotional support. Information. Leadership. Or a helping hand. As you move towards your goals, you will meet people who believe in what you are doing – and who want to help you in some way. Others will need help from you.

I am not saying you should be dependent. Waiting for someone else to give you what you need will not make you a leader. However, we are all interdependent. We all need each other's help to become leaders.

Think of groups whose members have helped each other become more successful. The Group of Seven. Junior Achievement, Rotary, Toastmasters. Alcoholics Anonymous. Athletic clubs or teams. Computer clubs. Business associations. Service clubs and support groups.

I sincerely believe in the ability of the individual. However, the power of working together far exceeds the power of working alone.

Using this Book in Your Organization

Some companies hire professional trainers or speakers to motivate, to bring in new ideas and skills, and to help them boost sagging spirits, revenues, and profits.

Speeches and seminars are a very good idea. (That's why I give them!) However, I believe that *many companies could be saving thousands of dollars annually* – by doing some of the training themselves. How? By using a book like this one.

Here's a suggestion: If you think people in your department would benefit from the ideas in this book, get everyone a copy. Have people read one chapter at home each week. Hold a weekly meeting at the office to discuss each chapter. Then apply what you learn. I believe that the results will pay off handsomely for your investment of time and money.

In the Special Tips section of this book, you will find more ideas on this subject. Look for the part entitled "Train Without a Trainer."

Taking Action

Review What You've Learned . . .

We are all leaders in one way or another.

The top leaders demonstrate these abilities:

- raising awareness and showing direction
- creating results
- helping others reach their goals
- achieving shared progress.

The most effective way to accomplish these outcomes is by working with the *leader-from-within*. This is the internally motivated, confident self within us that walks our talk, empowers others, and thrives on giving.

To lead from within, we must:

- Know what matters to us
- Have a vision of what is possible and the passion to express it
- Take risks to make it happen

- Communicate with others to make them part of the process
- Check progress and results.

These are two essential "tools" we use to create results:

Attitudes + Behaviour ⟹ Results

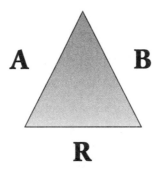

A   B

R

No one can create results by him/herself. We all need the encouragement, action, and leadership of others.

What we get out of life depends on what we put in. Ways to maximize results are continual learning, staying with projects (even when the effort far exceeds the return), setting SMART goals, and giving and receiving support.

. . . And Strengthen Your Leadership Muscles
(Exercises)

Experience comes from action. So don't just read these exercises. Do them – even just one. Start now. Have some fun with them, and watch your results grow.

1. Ask

    a) Rate these Ingredients of Leadership for their importance in becoming a leader. Use a scale of 1 (low) to 10 (high).

_____Personal values/ethics/   _____ Goal-setting
     knowing yourself   _____Knowledge of your field

_____Vision   _____General knowledge

_____Passion   _____Belief in yourself

_____Risk-taking   _____Desire to succeed

_____Communication skills   _____Doing what you love

_____Checking progress/results   _____Loving what you do

_____Hard work   _____Positive attitude

_____Persistence   _____Good with people

_____Associate with the right
      people

b) Compare your results to our Survey of Canadian Leaders, found in the Appendix.

c) Look at leaders around you. What makes them successful?

d) What kind of leadership are you providing: For yourself? Your family? Your company? Remember to consider: Are you/others happy? Are you getting the results you seek? What kind of environment are you creating?

2. Act

a) Set two goals this week: one personal; one business.
Each goal should follow the SMART formula.

S pecific   It should be clearly defined, not vague.

M easurable   It can be measured.

A ttainable   It is within my power to do.

R ealistic   It is possible and not just a pipedream.

T ruthful   It is something I really want to do.

b) Set yourself a penalty for not accomplishing your goals.

For your business goal: _____

For your personal goal: _____

(Note: Penalties are an incentive to encourage you to take action. They are *not* meant as punishment or to make you feel guilty.)

3. Associate

a) Identify three people you consider leaders – at work, in your community, in the media.

b) List some of the qualities that make these people leaders.

c) Talk to three people you know who have been successful. Ask them, "What three things have made you most successful?"

I recommend that you get a notebook to record your ideas and experiences. This will focus your thinking and help you remember what you learn.

> *[Personal growth] demands a lot of hard,*
> *conscious thinking. But it also involves the emergence*
> *of deeply buried feelings, revelations about oneself that*
> *are startling and unexpected. Know thyself is the*
> *name of the game, maturity the result.*
>
> – BETTY OLIPHANT, FOUNDER
> NATIONAL BALLET SCHOOL OF CANADA

KNOW
YOURSELF

Understanding Your Motivations

There are three things extremely hard:
steel, a diamond, and
to know one's self.
— BENJAMIN FRANKLIN

Plato said it in about 400 B.C.: "Know Thyself."

Shakespeare wrote it in *Hamlet*: "To thine own self be true."

Leadership experts such as Stephen Covey and Tony Robbins are recommending it today: "Know your own values. Listen to your heart. Find out what is important to you."

Why is knowing yourself so important to leadership?

Remember the Goals of Leadership

In the first chapter, I said that the goals of leadership are:

- to become more fulfilled
- to progress from where we are now to where we want to be
- to be more effective in creating results.

The only way you can achieve these goals is by knowing more about yourself; that is, by having answers to questions such as:

What makes you fulfilled?
What matters to you?
What do you want to create or do in your life?

Since results are created through *Attitudes* and *Behaviour*, you also need to know what you think and feel. What guides or drives you. What creates positive results in your life, and what does not. In essence, you need to know what *motivates* and enables you to succeed, whatever your goals may be.

That is what leadership from within is about – and it begins with knowing yourself.

WHAT DO YOU BELIEVE?

In his groundbreaking book *PsychoCybernetics*, Dr. Maxwell Maltz described his experiences with patients who underwent plastic surgery. He found that some patients, even after receiving a new physical appearance, went back to their old perceptions of themselves. As a result of his research, Maltz came to the following conclusion:

> *A human being always acts and feels and performs in accordance with what he imagines to be true about himself and his environment.*

What do you believe to be true about yourself? Do you see yourself as competent or incompetent? Worthy or unworthy? Powerful or a victim? Do you see yourself as having vision? Passion? Are you a risk-taker? Do you see yourself as able or unable – to express yourself or create the results you want in life?

If Maltz is right – and the more I study high achievers, the more I am convinced that he is 100 percent right – then you will "act, feel, and perform" according to these beliefs.

Next, consider what you "imagine to be true" about your environment.

- Do you see people as encouraging and supportive, or as unfriendly and uncaring?
- Do you believe that you have the power to do almost anything you choose, or that other people have power and you do not?
- Do you believe most people accept you the way you are, or judge what you say and do?
- Do you feel that your opportunities are virtually unlimited, or that you are limited by the economy or by fate?

None of these is right or wrong. However, if your beliefs are not positive, they will block you from being more fulfilled and successful.

If you are feeling inferior or afraid to do something, try this simple exercise:

Imagine something that seems impossible to you. Like inheriting $10 million from an unknown relative. Doing something super-human. Hitting eighteen holes-in-one in golf. Receiving an award for being the outstanding person in your entire industry. Take a few seconds to picture it clearly in your mind.

Now, try doing whatever you were scared to do before. See how this stretching of your internal self-image affects your performance in the outer world.

This process is called positive imaging or visualization. Many top athletes and performers use some form of it before major competitions or performances.

Knowing yourself starts with an awareness of your beliefs and motivations. Try this self-assessment. Ask yourself:

What are my most important
- attitudes
- behaviours
- values and beliefs
- fears?

What beliefs, habits, or memories drive me forward – or hold me back?

By recognizing what directs or controls you subconsciously, you can begin to make new choices.

(Tip: If you want to make rapid progress, start now. Take a couple of minutes. Pick two or three of these questions and jot down some notes. Do the rest when you have some time.)

In *PsychoCybernetics*, Dr. Maltz also concluded that we have a "guidance system" within us. This "goal-striving device" guides us towards living life more fully. Our subconscious helps us get there.

High achievers, for example, know they want to reach for the stars – and they go for it. Others are explorers, builders, or care givers – and they too must follow their own paths. If they do not follow this inner guidance or motivation, they start to die.

Do you have a calling or a vision?
What do you feel moved or driven to do?
What do you care most deeply about?

HAVE YOU CHOSEN YOUR FUTURE?

What is your "picture" or expectation of the future: for yourself or your family; your health; your career? How do you envision your community or society; your country; the environment?

Are your expectations of the future negative? If they are, watch out. Your subconscious and conscious choices, thoughts, and habits are all leading you in that direction. Quite literally, you will begin to get what you think about (if you *aren't* already!).

Now you could say, "Those aren't my only thoughts. I have dreams of improving. Hopes of going places. Of winning the lottery. Don't they count?" They do. But they are not enough. Dreams and vague hopes are not choices. In fact, they often mask underlying fears that your life is *not* going to get better.

A choice is a definite, conscious decision that leads to new attitudes and behaviour. It takes you away from the wishy-washy part of you that says "maybe" and "I hope for." You begin to say *no* to what you do not want – and *yes* to what you do.

The more clear choices you make, the more energy you direct towards your goal. It is the power of these consistent thoughts and actions that brings results.

Let's apply this to a practical example – like making dinner. You can dream about having a great meal. You can hope that someone will prepare it for you. But until you make some choices, you will still be hungry.

You could decide on what you want to make and cook your own dinner. You could ask your mother or a friend to do so. You could call up your favourite restaurant and book a table for 7:30. Or . . . I think you get my point. There are many ways to create the result you want. The choice is up to you.

This same idea holds true for finding a job. Creating a new product or business. Improving morale in organizations. Making local lakes and rivers clean enough to swim in. It's not enough to hope it will happen. You have to choose it – or you will lose it!

Take some time to think about what you "hope" will happen – but don't really believe *will* happen.

How important are these things to you? Is it worth making a choice and doing something about it?

Your choices influence others

Our power to influence others is far greater than we think. Most of us naturally follow each other's leads – in clothing and fashion, in music, in the cars we buy and the food we eat.

Others are affected by your energy, your words, and your actions. What you say to the courier or the cab driver, the salesclerk, your employees, or your boss has a ripple effect. Remember the old commercial:

You tell two friends. Then they'll tell two friends.
And so on and so on . . .

That's how it works. Each of us directly influences dozens of lives each day. Indirectly, without even thinking about it, we touch hundreds of people, whether positively or negatively.

Knowing yourself means increasing your awareness. It gives you the option to make conscious choices. It begins with asking yourself, "What do I want to create and experience today?"

Your choices draw people to you

When you make definite choices, you start attracting people by your behaviour. This can happen in many ways. Perhaps you speak your mind at a meeting. You voice an opinion on a phone-in radio show. You write a letter to the editor. Everywhere, people are watching and listening. They are looking for someone of like mind, someone who can express what they cannot. You become a leader.

Maybe you take it a step further. You are starting a business and invite someone to be your business partner. You need new staff and put an employment ad in the newspaper. You are running a workshop and you promote it on radio and television.

Others will be attracted by both what you choose to say and how you choose to say it. Think about whether your messages are clear or confused. Strong or weak. Caring or angry. Positive or negative. And remember: Watch how you feel, what you think, and what you want, because, to paraphrase the movie *Field of Dreams*, "if you choose it, they *will* come."

Do You Know What You Want and Need?

Most of us do not know what we want. I have seen it in business, in politics, and in relationships. We cannot even decide where to go or what to have for lunch!

As silly as this seems, it's actually quite important. By not choosing, we give up our power of choice. The choices are made by others. By not asking ourselves what we want, we miss the opportunity to be clear and to get what we need to satisfy us.

We do this because choosing is often not easy. When we make a decision, we listen to many voices within us. What our emotions want. What our head says is right. How much we should spend. What we should eat. What our values are.

Even simple choices bring up these ideas and feelings. Therefore it is important to make these small choices so we resolve the conflicts within us. By practising on the small ones, the larger choices in life become easier.

As I've said, knowing what you want helps you take care of your own needs. Here is a personal example:

I get very upset in traffic jams. So rather than set myself up to get angry, I avoid them. I leave earlier or later. If I have to travel at busy times, I may take a limo or a cab so somebody else does the driving. Because I value my own peace of mind, I do what I need to to stay out of heavy traffic.

By knowing your weaknesses, you can find others to help you make up for them. That way you build on strengths – yours, and those of the people you work with. The result is a better product, less struggle, and a win-win situation for everyone.

Consider what areas of your life could be improved through conscious choices.

- *Are you a morning person or a night hawk?*
  Do you try to do your most creative work at your *best* time of day – or your worst?

- *Do you feel better when you eat a certain diet or exercise regularly?*
  If so, do you do it?

- *Do you work best with people around – or by yourself?*
  Is your work environment set up for this? (e.g., Do you shut your door, or stop taking calls or visits, to give yourself the space you need?)

Learn what makes you most productive, happy, and fulfilled. Make choices that apply this knowledge effectively. Then watch your reactions and the results you get.

By the way, you're not bad or wrong if you don't make these choices. Life just works better when you do.

Make Decisions

- It's better to make the wrong decision than no decision.

- To get clear on what you want, write yourself a mission statement. Your main objective in life. Review it often.

- If you do not make decisions, you will keep thinking about them. You will become more fatigued, or stay awake at nights. Make decisions — and sleep better.

- We more often regret things we did not do than things we did.

- How do you decide? It's good to analyze the situation. It is also good to listen to your inner feelings. The best decisions are a combination of the two.

- Focus. The more you are focused, the less you will become confused. The less you are confused, the more you will accomplish.

- When you make a decision, stick with it. Unless it is causing someone pain or hardship, do not go back and question it.

- Life is full of decisions. Let your spouse make all the little decisions. You make the big ones. (Luckily, there are no big decisions!)

When in doubt because of conflicting advice, go with your own gut instinct. Think twice about every important decision, but also "consider the turtle. He makes no progress until he sticks his neck out."

— DENNIS MCDERMOTT

THE POWER OF SELF-IMAGE

Have you ever heard of successful people who lost everything, yet made it all back and were "on top" again in a very short time? How is that possible, when many people are not able to do it even once? I believe it's because they *know* they can do it. Having done it before, their self-image still tells them they are winners.

As Maxwell Maltz stated, what we believe to be true has a powerful effect on how we feel and act. Part of leadership, then, is breaking through these barriers in thinking, so that others can follow after us.

The story of the "four-minute mile" is a thrilling saga of how runners achieved "the impossible" by breaking two barriers, the physical barrier and the psychological barrier.

Is it possible for a human being to run one mile in four minutes or less? Until 1954, the answer was no. Commentators and athletes reasoned that the human body lacked the strength and the stamina to perform such a feat.

Then Roger Bannister became the first athlete to run a mile in under four minutes; 3:59.4, to be exact. The British runner broke the barrier at a meet in Oxford, England, on May 6, 1954. As a medical student, Bannister had taken the time to study not only the physiology of athletic movement, but also the psychology of performance.

Records, once broken, are often broken again and again. Six weeks later, John Landy of Australia shattered Bannister's record, running in 3:58.0. Then, at a monumental match between the two at the British Empire Games in Vancouver in August of 1954, Bannister raced against Landy and beat him. Both had again broken the four-minute mark.

The achievements of Bannister and Landy would lead to a whole series of sub-four-minute clockings. By the end of the 1960s, almost 200 men from over a half-dozen nations had broken the once seemingly impregnable barrier.

For generations, the "four-minute mile" was believed to be impossible. That is the image people had, of themselves and their environment. When Bannister broke through this barrier for himself, he actually broke through for others. All runners then knew it was possible.

David Niven, the well-known and popular actor, died of throat cancer in 1983. He could not speak before he died. But his last gestures were a smile and a "thumbs up" to those present.

Many people become depressed when they believe they are dying. They lose energy and the will to live. Others find renewed joy in everyday life. They report feeling more alive as a result of their condition.

What is the difference between someone living to die and someone dying to live? Why do some sixty-year-olds seem younger than the thirty-year-olds down the street? The answer lies in their self-image.

Self-image is learned

It is given to us by those around us. Parents. Teachers. Friends. The media. People say, "You're average." "You're stupid." "You're too old." From these simple words come the thoughts we live by — and say to ourselves. However, we can also cancel or change those thoughts. We have a choice.

When you change your "self-talk," your feelings change. So do your ideas about what you can have, do, or become. It expands your picture of what is possible in life. It encourages you (i.e., it brings you more courage) to take risks. It therefore helps you create better results. And all of these are communicated to others through your words and actions.

Just as Roger Bannister did for runners, you can help others shift to a higher level of attitude, behaviour, and results. It starts with improving your own self-image.

How do we improve self-image?

You may not have chosen it, but you are now responsible for the image you carry. Here are some steps you can take towards changing it.

Step 1: See yourself clearly.
Is the image you carry the image you want? If it is, then it is perfect. It

does not matter if you are a loser or a winner, a failure or a saviour. If you want it and feel fulfilled, be happy with it.

If you do not like your self-image, start by accepting yourself as you are. Acceptance promotes flexibility and caring, two qualities you will need to make a change.

Step 2: Decide what self-image you want.

I suggest you choose something that is "reasonable." Some of us have such high expectations for ourselves that we can't achieve them. If your desired self-image is unreasonable, you actually limit yourself – with guilt, frustration, and a sense of powerlessness.

What is reasonable? It's whatever you think it is. Can you really imagine accomplishing "it"? How long will it take? Are you prepared to do it?

Do not be afraid to set your goal high. But remember, you need to make progress towards it or you will feel depressed.

Step 3: Hold the new "picture" and live up to it.

Remind yourself frequently of your desired self-image. Find your passion or your inner drive to have it. Use exercises to build it. These could include:

- *Affirmations* – positive self-talk or statements that you say or write to yourself.
- *Visualization* – a "mental movie" of your new self-image that you run through in your mind's eye, while relaxing.
- *Quotes and pictures* – of how you want to be. Put these where you will see them. Beside your computer screen. In your wallet. On your bathroom mirror.
- *Physical exercises* – to build up your physical energy, stamina, and strength, and to give you a better feeling about yourself.
- *Specific activities* – to bring you closer to your goal. For example, if you want to build your muscles, lift weights. If you want to be a leader, do some of the exercises suggested in this book.

Start slowly. Build on small successes. Divert from old habits. Try new things. Start seeing and experiencing life from a new perspective.

Step 4: Seek out people who hold a similar picture – of themselves and you.
You can do this in person or through books and audio/video tapes. Check the Self-Help/Psychology and Leadership sections of your local bookstore or library. Get audiotapes from companies like Nightingale-Conant. Join groups in your community that inspire you and focus on personal development, vision, risk-taking, and communication.

Your friends are exactly the way you are – or would like to be. So if you have silly, dull, and foolish friends . . .

Watch who you hang around with. We are tremendously affected by the people around us. Our spouses. Parents. Friends. Co-workers. That is how most of our learning is accomplished. What they say and do rubs off on us. It doesn't matter whether they are depressed, angry, or uplifting, or whether they are penny-pinchers or risk-takers.

I know for certain that I would not be where I am now if I did not hang around the people I do.

I would not be running marathons if I had not joined the Fitness Institute – and chosen runners as my friends.

I would not be a professional speaker if I had not joined a local speakers club and become an active board member.

I would not be as successful a speaker if I did not belong to the National Speakers Association and go to their summer conference and winter workshops to meet hundreds of the world's top speakers.

And, despite the fact that I have not been a smoker for over twenty years, I would probably start smoking again if I started hanging around with people who do.

How Do We Learn About Ourselves?

First look at others

Many of us are reluctant to look at ourselves. We are afraid of what we will see. Of what we have or have not done.

One way to start is by getting to know others! Here are some tips:

- *Observe.* Watch people everywhere you go. Observe their behaviour and attitudes. In particular, look for people who seem to be comfortable or happy with themselves.

- *Communicate.* Ask people who are good at something why they have been successful. In sales. Management. Sports. Skateboarding. It doesn't matter what. Any successful person has qualities we can learn from.

- *Study.* Read about people in magazines, biographies, and autobiographies. Watch TV programs like A&E's *Biography*. Study successful people. Leaders. People who have excelled. Get to know what makes them tick — their attitudes, behaviours, talents, and weaknesses.

Now look at yourself

Create some space for yourself. Go somewhere quiet. Take a notebook. And relax; this is not a performance evaluation or an exam. You are just here to meet someone, perhaps for the first time.

Consider the following list, and jot down a few notes about:

Your past: accomplishments that you are proud of
Your strengths: abilities, skills, talents
Your weaknesses: limitations, fears, what presses your buttons
Your potential: what you feel you could do or be
What you care about: what you love to do, what you are gladly

committed to (even if you don't get paid for it)

What holds you back: beliefs; or something that hurts when you think about it

Your level of happiness: whether you are fulfilled, satisfied, at peace.

You don't have to do the whole list. Pick those that mean something to you.

Life isn't fair. Did you already find that out? It would be nice if it were. But I do not think it was supposed to be. In every part of life there is "good news and bad news."

The bad news here is that you are not perfect. There are many things you are not good at. The good news is you do not have to be.

In the school of life, there are two big lessons. The first is to get to know who you are. To see yourself clearly. To know what you can and cannot do, and to accept that.

The second is to discover what you can do with who you are.

> *God, give us grace to accept with serenity*
> *the things that cannot be changed,*
> *courage to change the things which should be changed,*
> *and the wisdom to distinguish the one from the other.*
> — REINHOLD NIEBUHR, *The Serenity Prayer*

Get to know your talents and skills

We all have talents or gifts; things that come easily to us and that we enjoy doing. If you want to be a leader, discover your *natural abilities* and use them to the fullest. They are the source of the "flow" and the vitality that propel the leader-from-within.

These talents will only take you so far, however. You also need to develop skills, or *learned abilities*.

I believe there is a system or a technique to everything in life. Even if you do not have a natural talent for something, when you find out "the system," you can learn how to do it. This applies to being a better golfer, scientist, or salesperson. Parent, spouse, or lover. Whatever. Begin by deciding what you want to be or accomplish. Then find someone who is experienced in that field and learn from them.

It is when you put these two together – natural talent with mastery of skills – that you will really become a leader.

> Michael Jordan, one of the all-time great basketball players, did not make the Varsity basketball team in his second year of university. He was not good enough. However, the coach of the team met Michael each day before class to work with him and helped him make the team the following year.
>
> Michael went on to become a leader for the world champion Chicago Bulls in the National Basketball Association. He is one of the highest scoring and highest paid players of all time.

So What Motivates You?

As I've said, a key part of knowing yourself is knowing what motivates you. What it is that makes you decide and act the way you do.

In the previous section, I described two ways that we are motivated. One I called the leader-from-within. The other, the leader-from-without. The first is moved by the desire to give, express, and serve. They have a certain confidence and security that guides their choices. The second is the opposite. The leader-from-without is motivated primarily by fear. Being without security and confidence, they seek fulfillment in the external world.

Both of these leaders are within us. And both, I believe, are motivated by needs.

Motivation = Unfulfilled needs

In the case of the outer-focused leader-from-without, the need is to get what we lack. This leader seeks satisfaction through people and things, positions and power. The result is a desire to shop and consume. To be famous and admired. To have authority and control.

The inner-directed leader is driven by the need to give. This leader has a fullness or abundance of creativity, energy, and love, and these must be shared or expressed.

The journey of life is a quest to fulfill these needs — and to discover which choices are most effective in accomplishing this. When the need is fulfilled, the desire goes away. We have reached our destination. But our needs have a funny way of coming back and moving us forward. Therefore it is important to choose a path that provides a continuing sense of satisfaction.

The beauty or happiness of life lies in the journey, not just in reaching our destination.

What is self-interest?

You may think of self-interest as your own personal interests. What you want, feel, need, do, and so on. However, if you were to serve only these interests, think of how much you would miss!

You would miss the warmth of loved ones. The abilities of co-workers. The support of team members. All of their interests also affect you. If they are not happy, strong, or fulfilled, if they are not talented, creative, and empowered, then they will not be able to contribute to your well-being.

The same is true for people throughout your organization, community, and country. For other countries. For the environment. Their well-being comes back to affect you, because we are all part of a "whole."

I believe that "self-interest" has three parts: my interests, your interests, and the interests of the whole.

The feeling is what counts

When you satisfy a need, you feel better. Getting a new computer. Helping someone. Making a great presentation. Closing a sale. The better you feel, the better you perform, and the better results you create.

These in turn reinforce your good feelings, and the cycle of success continues.

Feeling good is the real "bottom line." The purpose of everything else — profits, power, sex, money, fashion, TV, food — is to give you that feeling.

This provides a clue to having greater fulfillment. If you seek fulfillment rather than things, the things will take care of themselves.

"WHOA! Wait a second. That's not what the rest of society says. We've been taught since childhood that satisfaction comes from the things we get. From the power we hold. The people we control. The fame we get. Why is what you're saying so different?"

Good question. That is a natural reaction.

It *is* the way we have been educated and raised. We are an outer-focused culture. (That is part of the leadership-from-without way of thinking.) We are encouraged to want what we do not have. We believe that having it — consumer goods, position, fame, whatever — will bring us happiness. But that is only partly true. Things may help fill a need, but they do not ensure happiness. Happiness can *only* come from *within* us.

> Think about running your own business. You sweat and toil to get it started. You market like crazy to bring in the customers. For months on end it seems as if you will never have enough. You pray like heaven for business to come in. But the feeling of frustration grows as you look at your declining bank balance.
>
> Then something shifts. You become known. Prospects start to call. Business starts trickling, then flowing, in. It feels great for a time — but you start to worry. There are so many customers that you cannot meet the demand. You do not have enough hours to do the work. You pray like heaven that things will slow down. But the feeling of frustration grows as you look at how little time you have to enjoy yourself.

Sounds crazy. But it is true. The two situations are totally different, yet the feelings that resulted are the same. This is because what you focus on affects your experience. If you focus on what you do not have, you get frustrated. When you focus on what you do have, you get more happiness.

A similar thing happens with money and shopping. Most people are motivated to get more money so they can buy more things. But often, when they get what they thought they wanted, it does not satisfy them for very long. Then they are off looking for something more. This is because the "things" do not provide the satisfaction.

As I said earlier, every result or goal has two components – the tangible or physical thing you get, and the feeling you experience. For lasting satisfaction, focus on the experience.

By the way, I want to make it clear I am *not* against money or having things! But $$$ and possessions are not the be-all and the end-all (except if you do not have any!).

Giving vs. Getting

The egoist is looking for what the altruist
has found without looking for it.
　　　　　　　　– AUTHOR UNKNOWN

When we are looking for something outside ourselves, we are motivated by emptiness. We think we lack something, and are seeking to fill that gap.

When we give, on the other hand, we are motivated by a sense of fullness. We already have something – such as ideas, money, talent – which we then give to someone else. They then have more, and we have more good feelings as a result of giving.

Through helping, you enrich yourself. You discover how much you actually have. When you give out of a sense of plenty, you experience more satisfaction – even though you may actually have less of the food, money, or gifts you gave away.

So whatever you want, give it away . . . and you will get more of it.

We make a living by what we get.
We make a life by what we give.
　　　　　　　　– WINSTON CHURCHILL

Understanding Your Personality Type

*Am I not destroying my enemies
when I make friends of them?*
— Abraham Lincoln

Back home in Switzerland, I took a course on human behaviour at the University of Basel. From that moment on, it has fascinated me to see how different we all are, how we see and relate to the world in very different ways. Since coming to Canada, I have continued to study personality types.

Analyzing personalities can help us to know ourselves and others much better. How we think. How we act. Our beliefs and our perspectives on life.

I have found that people all over the world seem to believe two things:

1. We are "right" about how we see, think, and act. (Our religion, our country, our language, the food we eat, the art we like, and so on.)
2. Other people see life the same way we do — or at least they should!

But in fact, we all come at life differently. Some think things out logically; others are highly intuitive. Some are good at math and science, while others are natural artists or actors. There are those who love walking in the country, and those who love the hustle and bustle of city life.

In this chapter, I want to introduce you to the personality analysis. I think you will find it useful for knowing yourself better, and for understanding others.

Identifying Personality Types

The characteristics of human behaviour have been studied for centuries. About 400 B.C., Hippocrates developed a list of what are now called the "four medieval temperaments." Peter Drucker, Myers-Briggs (based on the work of Carl Jung), and many others have followed in his footsteps, having seen the value of understanding the human personality in more detail.

Some analysts divide our personalities into up to sixteen or more categories. However, most analyses boil down to four major types, which I will describe shortly.

Similarly, some psychologists use a twenty- or thirty-page questionnaire to identify your individual personality traits. However, I'm Swiss; I like to do things as simply as possible. So I developed my own personality analysis checklist (based on the work of others), which will take you about five minutes to complete.

The personality analysis

Take a few minutes to do the following simple self-assessment. You will learn some fascinating things about yourself in the process. You may also want to compare yourself to others you know – a significant other, your children, or your co-workers. I have included another copy of these pages in the Appendix for this purpose.

In the following lists, underline those words (or phrases) that describe you best in a *business* or *work situation*. Total your score for each group of words.

Group

A Reserved, uncommunicative, cool, cautious, guarded, seems difficult to get to know, demanding of self, disciplined attitudes, formal speech, rational decision-making, strict, impersonal, businesslike, disciplined about time, uses facts, formal dress, measured actions. **Total score:** _____

B Take-charge attitude, directive, tends to use power, fast actions, risk-taker, competitive, aggressive, strong opinions, excitable, takes social initiative, makes statements, loud voice, quick pace, expressive voice, firm handshake, clear idea of needs, initiator. **Total score:** _____

C Communicative, open, warm, approachable, friendly, fluid attitudes, informal speech, undisciplined about time, easy-going with self, impulsive, informal dress, dramatic opinions, uses opinions, permissive, emotional decision-making, seems easy to get to know, personal. **Total score:** _____

D Slow pace, flat voice, soft-spoken, helper, unclear about what is needed, moderate opinions, calm, asks questions, tends to avoid use of power, indifferent handshake, deliberate actions, lets others take social initiative, risk-avoider, quiet, go-along attitude, supportive, cooperative. **Total score:** _____

Write your total scores below:

A = _____　C = _____

B = _____　D = _____

Next, determine which groups are larger and by how much:

A vs. C: Which is larger?　　_____
　　　　　By how many points? _____

B vs. D: Which is larger?　　_____
　　　　　By how many points? _____

Filling in the personality grid

Now mark your results on the grid below:

To determine where you fit on the vertical axis, look at your A vs. C result. For example:

    If A was larger than C by 6 points, put a dot (•) at **A-6**.

    If C was larger than A by 5 points, put a dot (•) at **C-5**.

    If A and C are equal, put a dot (•) at "0," in the centre of the grid.

To find your place on the horizontal axis, use your B vs. D result.

    If B was larger than D by 4 points, put a dot (•) at **B-4**.

    If D was larger than B by 7 points, put a dot (•) at **D-7**.

    If B and D are equal, put a dot (•) at "0," in the centre of the grid.

In the grid below, draw an X where lines extending from your two points meet (as shown in the sample). The quadrant you're in indicates your personality type.*

Sample Grid

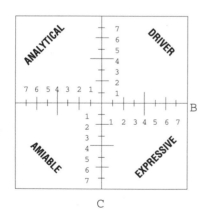 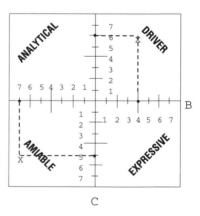

This sample grid shows the results for two different people: one is called a driver; the other is an amiable.

---

* These four personality types are adapted from *Personal Styles and Effective Performance*, by David W. Merrill and Roger H. Reid

Interpreting your results

Now that you know where you fit, let's find out what it means!

The following words describe each of the personality types. Read those that apply to you, and see how these words fit your image of your own personality. Then ask others what they think. It helps to get different perspectives.

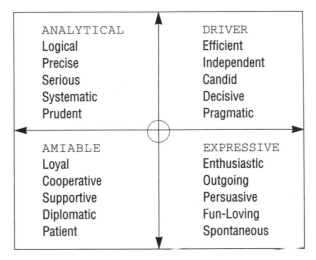

After considering your own personality, look at people around you. What personality types do they exhibit?

Remember that there is no right or wrong personality type. Different types simply think and act in different ways.

UNDERSTANDING THE PERSONALITY TYPES

Each personality has different needs, values, and motivations. Different levels of assertiveness and responsiveness. Here are some general insights into each type — and some tips to help you get through life a little more easily.

Note: In each category, I have included different names used by others to describe the same personality type. These are summarized in the table on page 66.

The Analytical

Also known as:
Melancholic
Thinker
Thought Man
Processor
Cognitive

The analytical person:

- wants to know "how" things work
- wants to be accurate, and to have accuracy from others
- values numbers, statistics, ideas
- loves details.

Analyticals fear being embarrassed or losing face. They also tend to be introverted and to hide their emotions from others.

The Amiable

Also known as:
Phlegmatic
Feeler
People Man
Helper
Interpersonal

The amiable person:

- wants to know "why?" (e.g., Why am I doing this?)
- wants to build relationships
- loves to give others support and attention
- values suggestions from others.

Amiables fear losing trust or having disagreements with others. While somewhat introverted, they also tend to display their emotions.

The Driver

Also known as:
Choleric
Director
Action Man
Boss
Behavioural

The driver:

- wants to know "what" (What will this do for me/the firm?)
- wants to save time
- values results
- loves being in control, in charge, doing things his/her own way.

Drivers fear giving up control. They tend to be extroverts, but do not like showing their emotions to others.

The Expressive

Also known as:
Sanguine
Intuitive
Front Man
Impulsive
Affective

The expressive person:

- wants to know "who" (Who else is involved; who else have you worked for?)
- values appreciation, applause, a pat on the back
- loves social situations and parties
- likes to inspire others.

Expressives fear being rejected. They are extroverts and usually show their emotions to others.

How Personality Theorists Have Described the Four Most Common Personality Types			
David W. Merrill and Roger H. Reid, *Personal Styles and Effective Performance*	Analytical	Amiable	Driver	Expressive
Hippocrates/Galen (Medieval Four Temperaments)	Melancholic	Phlegmatic	Choleric	Sanguine
Carl Jung	Thinker	Feeler	Director	Intuitive
Myers-Briggs	Introvert/ Thinker	Introvert/ Feeler	Extrovert/ Thinker	Extrovert/ Feeler
Peter F. Drucker	Thought Man	People Man	Action Man	Front Man
The Stuart Atkins LIFO System	Conserving-Holding	Supporting-Giving	Controlling-Taking	Adapting-Dealing
DISC	Steadiness	Compliance	Dominance	Influencing
Other well-known expressions	Processor Cognitive	Helper Interpersonal Supporter	Boss Behavioural Commander	Impulsive Affective Socializer

Strengths and Weaknesses of the Personality Types

Each personality type has different strengths and weaknesses. Here are some things to watch for in yourself, and in the people you work with.

Type	Strengths	Potential Weaknesses
Analytical	Thinking	Excludes feelings from decision-making
	Thorough	Goes too far; perfectionist
	Disciplined	Too rigid or demanding of self/others
Amiable	Supportive	Tends to conform to wishes of others
	Patient	No time boundaries; things do not get done
	Diplomatic	Not assertive or direct
Driver	Independent	Has trouble cooperating with others
	Decisive	Does not take time to consider other perspectives
	Determined	Domineering; too focused on doing it "my way"
Expressive	Good communicator	Talks too much
	Enthusiastic	Comes on too strong
	Imaginative	Dreamer; unrealistic

There is an old saying that "your greatest strength is also your greatest weakness." The above chart shows why this is so.

When any personality trait is too strong, it becomes excessive. Too much thinking, too much talking, too hard-driving, or being too friendly – any of these can be liabilities.

One way to deal with this is by developing balance. We all have traits from each personality group. By developing those that are currently weak, you will have strengths on all sides. You will be able to see situations from other people's perspectives. You will also be able to see the strengths and weaknesses of each.

The more integrated you are – that is, the more you are able to blend all styles – the better leader you will be. This will give you the flexibility to hold many positions, each requiring different personality skills. Seeing different perspectives, you will be more creative and able to solve problems more easily.

You will also be a better manager. Every organization needs a variety of talents – communicators, thinkers, doers, and support people. One of the strengths of a top manager is the ability to spot who can do what well, and to combine all these talents on their team.

Four people can stand on the same spot, but see four different views. One sees only an ocean, another only mountains; one sees mountains to the left and ocean to the right, and the last sees mountains on the right . . .

To see what another sees, you must not only be in the same spot. You must look in the same direction.

Understanding and Working with Others

When working or communicating, we need to find ways to "connect" with others. Apart from a common language, we need to share interests and terminology to understand what the other is saying. (If you have ever attended your spouse's office party, you know what I mean!) In the same way, we must work to bridge our differences in personality.

The following rule generally holds true:

The further away you are from someone on the personality grid, the more difficult it is to relate to them.

For example, a highly analytical person will likely find it difficult to work with someone who is very expressive. The same conflict could occur between a driver and an amiable. This is because their ways of thinking and working are quite different.

The driver tends to speed his/her way through life. Friendship takes a back seat to efficiency. The amiable, who is more laid back, takes time to make and nurture friendships. The analytical gets along well with other thinkers. But a gregarious expressive who talks a lot may rub the analytical the wrong way.

Most of the time, we do not have the luxury to choose. We must work with all personality types. To do this effectively, you will need to:

- *Observe.* Listen and watch for personality cues; be open to some-one else's style, values, and perspective.
- *Adapt.* Find common ground with someone who is different; this could be your speed of speaking or the terms you use (e.g., talking about facts vs. feelings).
- *Connect.* Watch for body language and get feedback from others to see if you are being understood; check your own thoughts/ feelings. Do you feel harmony or discord?

The objective is to understand and relate to all other personality types. That is when communication clicks and working together works best.

If you want to learn more about personality types, I recommend two books: *Personal Styles and Effective Performance*, by David W. Merrill and Roger H. Reid and *Social Style/Management Style*, by Robert and Dorothy Bolton. See the Appendix for full references.

> *You are how you are. You behave how you feel.*
> *Behavioral changes are outside changes.*
> *They will occur instantly, but won't last —*
> *unless you also feel change from within.*
> — PETER URS BENDER

TIPS FOR YOUR TYPE

For the Amiable:
- Speed up with *"fast"* people
- Talk more, listen less
- Take control occasionally; be assertive
- Take some risks

For the Analytical:
- Speak more and smile more
- Show appreciation and personal interest
- Relax; share information and be open to others
- Remember: Enthusiasm will not kill you . . .

For the Driver:
- Slow down with *"slow"* people
- Take time to listen to the ideas of others
- Hold back from dominating; relinquish some control
- Show more patience and act more relaxed

For the Expressive:
- Listen more; slow down, relax
- Write things down; set specific goals
- Check details and stay calm
- Learn to concentrate

THE VALUE OF THE PERSONALITY ANALYSIS

Here are some ways the personality analysis can help you become a leader:

- *Increased self-acceptance.*
  You will begin to accept more of your strengths and your weaknesses.
- *Improved awareness.*
  You will recognize where your strengths can become weaknesses.

- *More perspective.*
  You will be able to see (and have more understanding of) different sides of yourself and others.
- *Greater choice.*
  Knowing different personality qualities, you will be able to develop the ones you want.
- *More understanding and ability to work with others.*
  You will see the strengths and needs of people around you.
- *Enhanced personal growth.*
  You will feel more balanced, more integrated, and whole.

Use this information wisely

Presidents, entrepreneurs, and top leaders in every field come from all four groups. No personality type is right or wrong. However, certain types may fit certain jobs better than others. For example:

Analyticals are well-suited to jobs like accounting or research.
Drivers may reach high rank in the Armed Forces.
Amiables would make good social workers or counsellors.
Expressives can be successful as entertainers or marketing/sales
    executives.

Be sure to use personality information wisely. Do not use it to limit your own choices, judge people, or hold them back. Help yourself and others find the jobs and positions – those that are most suited to your (or their) personality – and then use these qualities to get ahead!
    Here are some ways to do that:

Be aware that people of a different personality type must do things differently to create the best results.

Work on your weaknesses and utilize your strengths.

If the personality type described in this book does not sound like you, ask yourself: Am I hiding another part of my personality? (You may have decided that being a driver, or being open with your emotions, is not acceptable.) Is it time to open up that side of yourself?

Coach others to develop other sides of themselves.

Include all personality types on your team, project, or in your organization. In particular, make sure you have members who are strong in the areas in which you are weak.

Identify your own leadership style. Do not try to become someone you are not. Be who you are and build on it! However, if you want to lead people with different personality types, you must adapt your style or they will not relate to you.

Make sure your personality "needs" are satisfied and fulfilled.

Find ways to work effectively with personality types that anger or upset you. Look for value in how they act. See some part of yourself in them. "Try on" their personality type. Maybe some aspect of it will benefit you.

Do you live a split life?

The first time you filled out the personality analysis, I asked you to do it for a business or work situation. Now I suggest you do it again. This time, use your *personal* side. Underline those words that describe how you are at home or with friends. (See the Appendix for another copy of the Personality Analysis.)

Many of us show different sides of our personality at work from what we show at home. In fact, we live split lives. We choose different goals, values, and ethics, and different ways of expressing ourselves. This is why some people are not fulfilled in business — because they do not believe they can be "themselves." See how different *your* personal and business personalities are. Can you bring them closer together?

THE PERSONALITY OF YOUR ORGANIZATION

Organizations are reflections of their leaders. Leaders' personalities come through in the people they choose, their management styles, and the attitudes and behaviour they display. As a result, organizations have their own personalities, too.

Let's use IBM and Apple as examples.

In the 1980s, these two companies reflected sharp differences in personality. IBM was "Big Blue" — the old-style, rigidly structured, traditional multinational organization. Apple was the new kid on the block. The upstart. Small and flexible. Started by a couple of computer hackers in their garage.

These personalities pervaded the two organizations. IBM used DOS — an analytical-style operating system. You had to know the computer language to operate it. Apple was known for its "amiable," user-friendly, drop-down-window-style operating system. IBMers had to use difficult-to-learn keyboard codes. (The "F" keys on computer keyboards.) Applers had the easy-to-use "mouse."

The TV commercials of both companies reflected these images. So did their management styles, working environments, training, and software/hardware development processes.

Consider the personality of the organization you are in. Does it work well for you? Do you work well within it? Can you see the benefits of its operating style? How could it be changed to better suit the employees in it? How could you adapt your personality to work better? Is it time to change, or leave, because you no longer "fit"?

Leaders cast long shadows.
If you don't like the results you are getting –
look carefully in the mirror. Every time I have done so . . .
inevitably I have found I was the source of the problem.
That is both the sobering reality – and a huge opportunity.

– DON McQUAIG, PRESIDENT,
MICA MANAGEMENT RESOURCES

PERSONALITIES OF YOUR CLIENTS

In one of my recent seminars, a middle-manager described a "very difficult client" he had to deal with. The client had a hard-driving, "I want it done my way" approach to work. She was well-known in the company for the problems she created.

Shortly after the manager joined the company, he was assigned to this account. His co-workers began to chuckle, knowing what lay ahead for him. It turned out, however, that he was very successful in working with her. When asked why, he said, "I dealt with her in the manner I thought she wanted or needed. It worked. She knew I could see her perspective."

If you have a client or customer you find hard to deal with, try looking at their personality type. See if there is some way you can work with them by adapting to their style.

That does not mean you should de-value yourself or your own style. It simply means you can gain from listening to your client – both their verbal and non-verbal messages – and serving them the way they want to be served.

Make it one of your goals to understand people. Also understand that the only person you can actually change is yourself. If you want to sell, coach, negotiate, or be with others, you have to be yourself *and* become like them.

WHAT BLOCKS YOU FROM KNOWING YOURSELF?

If Plato, Shakespeare, Stephen Covey, and Tony Robbins (to name but a few) all say "know yourself," then why don't we do it more often?

If I had the answer to that, I would be a multi-millionaire! I do have, however, some clues to the attitudes and behaviour that hold us back.

Past experience and guilt.
Sometimes we feel guilty about changing the way we live. For example, if you were raised with a strong work ethic, it can be hard to justify taking time off. Or if you were taught that making money is greedy or

selfish, then it can stop you from being prosperous in business. All of us live with these kinds of beliefs inside.

That can be rough. Often, it turns into a catch-22: you feel guilty if you do, and guilty if you do not. I do not have a perfect answer on what to do, but I encourage you to break out of that cycle of guilt.

Knowing yourself means questioning all that you have been taught before. That does not mean giving up your values. It means considering them in light of what you know today, and seeing if they are still what's best for you.

Find someone who can help you see things objectively. Are your desired goals and your values really in conflict? What was accepted in the past may no longer be valid today. Make your goal *both* freedom from guilt and excellent results.

A Need to be "Right."

If we believe there is only one right way — our way — then those who are different must be wrong!

Many of us were taught that to be right is good, and to be wrong is bad. This was reinforced by the rewards and punishments we received — at home, in business, and in our religions. As a result, we have become obsessed with being "right." But what does that mean?

In some countries, like Canada and the United States, the "right" handshake is one with a firm grip and strong pressure. In other places, such as Southeast Asia, a "limp" handshake is correct. Making eye contact with your boss in India is a no-no; it is a sign of disrespect. The opposite is true in the West.

Some men see being caring or compassionate as wrong. For some women, it is being too strong or powerful. "Being right" (or wrong) has also been associated with our dress styles, our accents, our wealth or lack of it, and our tendencies to accept authority or be independent.

These kinds of beliefs block us from knowing ourselves. Our fear of being wrong makes us conform to someone else's code of behaviour. It can lead to our becoming rigid, argumentative, unwilling to admit errors, and even dishonest.

Start to question whether "being right" is helping you – or stopping you – from finding the results and fulfillment you seek.

Fear of change.

Most of us resist change. We don't want to let go of what we have. We fear it means we are wrong or we have failed. That is uncomfortable to accept.

Try switching your thinking. Instead of seeing change as a sign of failure or weakness, see it as a sign of strength. Courage. Opportunity.

Ask yourself if you are getting the results you want. If you aren't, don't get stuck on the way you have always done things. Decide to find a better way.

> *When one door of happiness closes, another opens;*
> *but often we look so long at the closed door that*
> *we do not see the one which has opened for us.*
>
> – HELEN KELLER

Time and work pressure.

The leader-from-without has all sorts of ways to keep us from finding the leader-from-within. Having too little time or too much work are two such ways. It takes time to know yourself. To reflect and decide what matters to you.

Don't let these pressures block you! Many people have gone to their graves saying, "I will do it tomorrow."

Start today. Pick an idea in this chapter that you want to consider. Clear five minutes at the start or end of the day, and go to a quiet room. Ponder it while walking to the store. Or take this book to the washroom and spend an extra five minutes in there!

Check your "results" at the end of the day. If you did not take the time, decide to find it tomorrow. Do whatever is required to begin getting out of the time-work rat race.

Lack of awareness.

The pressures and stress of daily life often stop us from knowing ourselves. This is one reason why many people do not really know what they love to do. They are out of touch with what they care about – and with the effects these pressures can have on their bodies and minds. We often hear about medical problems such as ulcers and heart attacks that seem to happen "all of a sudden." There may be warnings of them beforehand, but we are just not aware.

Begin to notice your upset thoughts and feelings, as well as any tightness or pain in your body. Do not block them out. They are like the red oil light in your car – a sign that something is wrong and needs correcting. Use these signs as a stimulus for change.

A lack of awareness also prevents us from knowing the power we have within. Our talents and vision. Our image of ourselves is often very small.

Stop saying, "I can't do it." "I'm only his wife." "I'm just a small-town boy." "We're Canadian." "There is nothing I can do." "I'm too old to learn."

Believe that you *can* do it. Look for stories of people who "did it." Pray for help if that works for you. Whatever you need to do to believe you are worthy and able, do it.

Fear of making a decision.

Many people do not like making decisions. They are afraid of the change that is involved, the work they will have to do, or the results they might get.

What they forget is that *not* doing something is also a decision. It is a decision not to change. But there are still consequences.

If you continue doing what you are doing, you will probably get where you are going. Where are you headed?

Lack of specific goals.

Do you have too many things you want to do? Are you not getting any of them done? It can be hard making a choice. However, the fact is you *cannot* do everything at once.

Try this instead.

Decide on one or two activities per week, to start with – and commit yourself to doing them.

You might also want to try a longer test project. See how this works for you:

Decide on one project you want to do. Set a specific time period to complete it; twenty-one days is a good length. Make an agreement with yourself to do it. Put something in writing if you have to. (Some schools I know are doing this. They have students sign "contracts" to complete projects. It seems to increase their motivation and commitment.)

Now put the rest of the things you would like to do aside. You can always come back to them at the end of the test. But for this time period, see what you can accomplish by focusing your energy on that one thing.

Lack of options.

Sometimes it seems like there is *nothing* we can do. Know the feeling?

But let me tell you: there is always *something* you can do. You always have options. But it is going to take change. In attitude, behaviour, or both. Are you prepared to do it?

Tony Robbins began his climb to success while he was living in a 400-square-foot bachelor apartment. He had to do his dishes in the bathtub because the place didn't even have a kitchen.

"I started out," he says, "feeling sorry for myself. Feeling nothing could change. Being mad at the world and my past.

"But fortunately, I was able to change. And the change came from not being willing to settle for that any more. Knowing that inside I was much more than I was living: mentally, emotionally, and spiritually. And I was able to find my passion."

From these beginnings, Robbins went on to become one of the world's most dynamic professional speakers — with two best-selling books, the best-selling audiotape program of all time, and nine companies with annual revenues of $50 million.

Source: *Personal Power II: The Driving Force* (video), by Anthony Robbins.

Are you trapped in your own "400-square-foot apartment" or some other "box" in life? Then it's time to make a choice.

Choose to get better. Whatever that means for you. Next, take stock of what resources you have. What you can do to move ahead. What talents you have. Who you know. Who you can ask for guidance. Start building on what you have — and do not stop until you get where you want to go.

The lowest ebb is the turn of the tide.
— HENRY WADSWORTH LONGFELLOW

Fear of taking risks.
That is what change is — a risk. "If I do this, will I be better off than I am now? Is it worth what I have to give up?"

In my observation, anyone who does anything in life has taken risks. Success was not due primarily to their brain capacity. It came from the challenges they took on.

Ask yourself: "What progress have I made in the last three months? Have I taken any risks?" Take some. Start small or large, it's up to you.

Think about what you have to gain. Like you did when you started dating. Your stomach was probably upset, like mine was. You may have had cold, clammy hands. Maybe you could barely say "hello." But somehow you knew the risk was going to be worth it. (I hope it was!)

Low self-confidence.
Confidence is something we all lack at times. So try this: "Fake it until you make it." That's right. Act as if you have it, and you will get more. Shoulders back. Chin up. Smile. Your posture will signal to your brain that you are a winner. Your smile will signal it to others. Even if you are scared out of your tree, you will still be a winner — because you made a decision, took the risk, and did what you believe in.

The only choice or risk I am asking you to take at this stage is to get to know yourself. Look inside. Find out how you feel. Consider whether you are satisfied, and what more you would like to experience. In coming chapters, we will handle the rest.

The goal is to be fully yourself – instead of what others have tried to make you be or keep you from being.

The more you accept yourself, the more you will help others be who they are. And the more they will teach you that you are okay.

Believe in a great future within you and that you have talents and life skills that you have not dreamed of yet.

Don't let anyone persuade you otherwise – no matter how subtle or implied. Regardless of your situation, just don't believe it. Let others say or do what they want – you don't have any control over that.

The important thing is don't let what others say or do upset your fundamental belief in yourself.

– JOHN WILDMAN, PRESIDENT, THE FITNESS INSTITUTE

Taking Action

Review What You've Learned . . .

Attitudes + Behaviour ⇒ Results

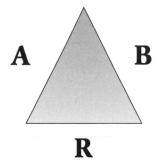

Attitudes
- Look at your beliefs, attitudes, behaviour, self-image; what is working and what is holding you back?
- Be aware of personality type – yours and those of others.

- Know what you want and need.
- See the value of different opinions, perspectives, skills.
- Listen to your thoughts and feelings.

Behaviour
- Go in the direction that will give you the most out of life.
- Do what you are best at.
- Acquiring "things" does not ensure "happiness"; go for both!
- Don't let weaknesses hold you back or make you upset. Find others who can do what you can't.
- Learn from/eliminate the little things that make you mad.
- Make decisions.

Results
- Feel motivated to do more, yet happy with what you have and your situation.
- Get positive results and feel fulfilled.

. . . And Strengthen Your Leadership Muscles
(Exercises)

1. Ask
a) When do I feel best? Worst? Most peaceful/content? Happiest? Angriest?

b) How fulfilled did I feel today? Ask this at the end of each day and rate yourself on a scale of 1 (low) to 10 (high).

c) In what situations do I shy away from taking leadership?

d) What do I really care about?

e) What are the five best things about my company?

f) Rate yourself on each of the Ingredients of Leadership.
   (S = Strong   M = Medium   W = Weak)

_____ Personal values/ethics/   _____ Goal-setting
         knowing yourself   _____ Knowledge of your field
_____ Vision   _____ General knowledge

_____ Passion   _____ Belief in yourself
_____ Risk-taking   _____ Desire to succeed
_____ Communication skills   _____ Doing what you love
_____ Checking progress/results _____ Loving what you do
_____ Hard work   _____ Positive attitude
_____ Persistence   _____ Good with people
_____ Associate with the right
        people

2. Act

a) Set two goals this week· one personal, one business.

   (Remember: The goals should be SMART:
   Specific. **M**easurable. **A**ttainable. **R**ealistic. **T**ruthful.)

b) Set yourself a penalty for not accomplishing your goals.

For your business goal: _____

For your personal goal: _____

c) Try on a different personality today. If you are analytical, you
   could try being expressive. If you are a driver, try being amiable.

3. Associate

a) Identify three people you believe "know themselves."
b) Spend time with some of these people. If you don't know them
   personally, read about them. Listen to them on tape. Study them.
c) Talk to someone today about "knowing yourself." Share your
   ideas and ask for theirs. Also ask for their perceptions of you. (I
   bet you will get some very interesting feedback!)

Have the courage of being your genuine self,
of standing alone and
not wanting to be somebody else.
— LIN YUTANG

HAVE VISION AND PASSION

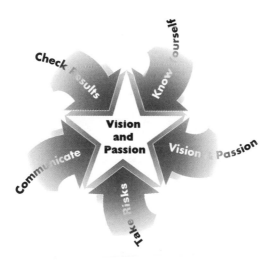

Leading with Vision

We are such stuff as dreams are made of.
— SHAKESPEARE, *A Midsummer Night's Dream*

Vision is the stuff of our dreams. Passion is our energy to make it real. The two go together like a horse and rider. In the mind of one is the goal. In the power of the other lies the means to get there.

What Is Vision?

Vision is a mental picture of the future. An idea of what is possible but has not yet happened.

There are at least three types of vision. Each holds a different picture of the future.

1. *Probable future*: What we can expect to happen if we continue as we are now.
2. *Desired future*: What we'd most like to have happen.
3. *Catastrophic future*: What could happen if things get worse or something really bad occurs.

Leadership deals with all three types of vision. Seeing where we are headed. Deciding where we want to go. And avoiding the problems or catastrophes that could befall us.

Vision is all around us

Vision is often seen as strange or weird. Something only saviours or crazy people get.

Nothing could be further from the truth. Everybody has vision. It is essential to life. You would not be sitting where you are right now if you didn't have it.

Say, for example, you are in an office. It is located several miles from where you live. How did you get there? While you were at home, you had an idea of "going to the office." That "vision" guided your choices and actions of where to go and how to get there. Other people's visions created the building you are sitting in, the car or public transportation you travelled on, and so forth.

Vision is so much a part of everyday life that we take it for granted. Here are a few examples that you may have experienced:

On your first date: Dreams of a long-term relationship, marriage, and children.

At your first job: Visions of what you'd like to accomplish, or the kind of company you want to build.

While out of work: Ideas for new businesses you want to start.

Vision is a tool used by everyone who ever wanted to create something. But it is particularly important for leaders.

By definition, a leader is "out in front." Going new places. Doing what others have not yet done. Leading the way for others. What leads the leader is vision. Leaders see what's possible – the solution, the victory, the sale, the opportunity – and work to make it a reality.

Vision is not always positive

Most people think of vision as creating a better future. But it is not always so.

- When we worry, we create a picture of future problems (based on our past experience).

- When we consider our financial future – as an organization, a family, or a country – sometimes it can look pretty bad.

- When we forecast the weather, we don't just see sunny days. We may see impending storms, floods, and hurricanes.

- When we make environmental predictions, many see disasters looming due to pollution, holes in the ozone layer, or global warming.

These are all a part of what vision can show us. Sometimes it is hard to face. The future can look quite bleak.

One of the qualities you need to develop in becoming a leader is a willingness to face these negative visions. To look at where you are headed when you would rather not see. Then to take action in order to avoid or prevent future problems.

Leadership – even from within – is often not easy. The challenge is to turn these potential hardships into opportunities for progress.

WHERE DOES VISION COME FROM?

Our pictures of the future are influenced by many sources. Past experience. Information and facts we read. Feelings we have. People we hear or meet.

In some cases, vision is a left-brain, logical extension of what we currently know. For example, say you are a salesperson. Your sales in one city are $100,000 and you have a vision to expand. If you open up in ten more cities of similar size, you could potentially gross $1 million. That makes logical sense.

More often, vision also involves the right brain, bringing new insight, new awareness into what is possible. An example of this was Einstein's discovery of the Theory of Relativity. (Don't worry, I'm not going to try to explain it.) As the story goes, Einstein was relaxing outside one day.

In his mind's eye, he was mentally walking up a sunbeam. Then "wham!" The idea came to him. Where it came from is anybody's guess.

The type of vision I want to focus on here is a combination of these two. I will call it "whole brain" vision. It combines:

- logic and intuition
- thoughts and feelings
- past experience and future potential
- the practical and the "impossible."

Whole brain vision startles us. It shakes us up. It is logical, but also somehow magical. It brings insight and ideas of wonderful new inventions or solutions to problems. It also helps us shape our world.

Christopher Columbus believed that the Earth was round. He had such confidence that he sailed across the sea — while his friends told him he'd fall off the edge. Why did he think he could do it?

Thomas Edison persisted with his vision and created the electric light — even though he "failed" some 10,000 times before succeeding. What was it that led him to continue?

Alexander Graham Bell knew the telephone would work. Ted Turner knew he could create a global satellite television network. Both were told they were crazy to even try.

There is something within that guides us. It comes as a desire to grow or improve. It embodies our hopes and ideals. It gives us a sense of purpose. In dreams or flashes of insight, vision brings us images of what is possible. It waits for us to put the idea into action.

Vision starts with knowing yourself

Sometimes vision comes as a blinding flash. But most of the time, it results from our normal ways of thinking. Architects dream of building new buildings – not usually of designing new computer programs. Business people think about how to grow their businesses – not about flying to the planets or the stars.

It is therefore important to start with knowing yourself. What is important to you? What are your values? What do you want to do? These fundamental beliefs will direct your mind to create your vision.

Whether you want to heal the sick, or find a new way to create war, your desire will lead to visions about how to accomplish what you choose.

For me, leadership is about having a positive vision and making it real.

Why Is Vision Important?

- *It creates our reality.*
  Our vision of what is possible guides our choices. Our choices guide our actions. And so we build the world.

  Tomorrow, for example: Will the entrepreneur in you create the new work you've always wanted – or will you go back to a job you've cursed for so many years? Will you do pioneering research on a cure for AIDS or cancer – or continue working as a frustrated lab technician?

  It depends on your vision.

- *Vision shows us where we are headed.*
  It's important to look ahead. If you are headed towards financial collapse, you need to know before it happens. If your company must double its staff to handle a new contract you're about to receive, vision helps you prepare for that.

- *It helps us fulfill our desires.*
  Vision gives insight, information, and ideas about how to accomplish our goals. How to design that new bridge. What products and services to sell when starting a new business. Ways to cut costs while increasing employee morale. (Now there's a vision!)

- *Vision gives us new direction.*
  Sometimes we get a vague "sense" that we need to take a new direction — like leaving our job, starting a new career, or changing relationships. It takes time to clarify who, what, when, where, and why.

  Other times it is like Ebenezer Scrooge in Dickens' *A Christmas Carol.* One night he went to bed as usual. The next morning he woke up a changed man.

- *It helps us make specific choices and decisions.*
  Once a vision is identified, specific goals or targets can be set to accomplish it. You can then determine how much time and money, how many people, and what types of skills you will need to complete the project.

- *Vision provides motivation and inspires us to keep going.*
  Why do Olympic athletes train day after day, year after year? Why did Terry Fox run his Marathon of Hope? Because of vision.

  All of us start activities — a healthy diet or a new course of study, for example — because of the end result we have in mind. Our vision needs to be strong enough to carry us through. Otherwise, we will stop short of the goal.

- *It focuses us.*
  Are you trying to go in twenty-five different directions at once? Then try this. Choose one vision you have had and act on it. It will focus your thoughts and actions and the way you use your time.

- *Vision moves us towards what we want rather than what we do not want.*
  Many people say "I don't like this" and "I don't like that." Their minds and energies are always focused on what they do not have. Vision rechannels your energy towards what you have chosen to create.

- *It draws us forward and takes us beyond obstacles.*
  Say you live in a cold climate and the winter is freezing your rear end off. You decide to get away from it all and drive to Florida.

  As your car rolls out of the driveway, you get a flat tire. You may swear like crazy. But do you stop? No. You do whatever you need to get that tire fixed. Fast. The vision of that Florida sun keeps drawing you forward.

  The stronger your vision, the smaller the problems will seem along the way. If the vision is not strong, the problems will take over.

- *Vision gives meaning and purpose.*
  It helps us see the end result of our efforts. It gives us the answer to "why?" — a reason for doing what we do.

When we see the whole vision, we begin to see how all the parts fit together. How the little things, the details, make a difference. Like the cleanliness of washrooms to the success of a McDonald's restaurant. Or the importance of each brick in the building of the cathedral.

Who Has Vision?

Everyone does. You do. You have visions about where you'd like to go on vacation. What you'd like to accomplish in life. Who you might fall in love with, and so on. If you ever think about "what could be," that's the beginning of vision.

Vision is both a natural talent and a skill you can develop. Some people are better at it than others because they are more open to creative ideas. But for anyone, vision grows with practice.

If you want to spot others who have vision, look for:

- *These who see opportunities* — e.g., entrepreneurs.
  They see solutions where others see problems. They see ways to create new products, services, and businesses.

- *Those who develop "something from nothing"* – e.g., musicians, artists, writers, inventors.
  Their raw material is their creativity. Their thoughts and feelings. They have words, pictures, and sounds inside that they translate into something others can see, hear, or touch.

- *Those who see potential for growth* – e.g., teachers, coaches.
  They recognize your potential – and help you reach it.

- *Those with imagination* – e.g., children.
  When a child looks at a plate of food and sees skyscrapers, fire engines, and rocket ships, that's vision! They are seeing everyday things through new eyes.

- *Those with intuition* – e.g., people who trust hunches or gut feelings, and the spiritually minded.
  Some people have a sense of future events before they happen. Others get ideas about what to do, what to say, or where to go, and the results show they were right.

- *Those who see beyond where we are now* – e.g., explorers.
  Most of us look at what is around us and think that's all there is. Others think of distant places. New lands. Exploring new ways of thinking, relating, learning.

On May 25, 1961, U.S. President John F. Kennedy delivered an address to a joint session of the U.S. Congress. He titled it "Urgent National Needs" and in it he made a breathtaking announcement: The United States would put a man on the moon and return him safely before the decade was out.

It was both a race to beat an opponent and a challenge to achieve an impossible dream.

Up to that time, the U.S. space program had been inferior to that of the Soviet Union, its rival not only in military preparedness but also in space exploration. With Sputnik, the U.S.S.R. was the first nation in space. However, by harnessing both national pride and the resources of the Federal Treasury, the United States launched Project Apollo and undertook a series of manned flights.

When Kennedy made his announcement, there were many in the space program who didn't believe it was even possible. Yet nine years later, the dream became a reality.

On July 19, 1969, the Apollo 11 lunar module set down on the face of the moon. Stepping onto the lunar surface the next day, Commander Neil Armstrong said memorably, "That's one small step for [a] man, one giant leap for mankind." Four days later, the three Apollo astronauts were safely back on Earth. It was a triumph of human ingenuity and intelligence, of vision and determination.

How Can You Develop Vision?

Here are some key steps in developing your ability to have vision.

1. *Begin with the end in mind.* – Stephen Covey
   Start by asking yourself a few fundamental questions:

   - What do I want?
   - Where am I headed?
   - What would I like to create or achieve?

2. *Get clear on the results you want to see.*
   The previous step gave you a general idea of what you want. Now make it specific. In your mind's eye, begin to picture:

   - The physical conditions you envision.
     For example, you are starting a new company. Do you need a factory or a small office? One employee or hundreds? Is your vision to sell to your local community or around the world?

   - The working conditions you want to create.
     How are people treating each other?
     How do you feel at the end of each day?

The most successful individuals and companies have quite clear visions about what they want to accomplish. The clearer yours is, the more likely you will be to accomplish it.

3. *Make it a shared process.*
   Vision starts with you. But few of us work totally alone. What you want also affects – and is affected by – your family. Your association, community, and company. And everyone involved has their own unique vision.

   When working with others, it is important to combine these visions to create a shared mission that answers the question: "What do *we* want?" This is your purpose for being together; the desired result of your shared efforts.

   You cannot create a mission for other people. It has to come from within *them*, because they need their own vision (and passion) to drive them forward.

4. *Consider what actions will make it real.*
   Having clarified your vision, now look at actions. What do you have to do to create the results you want?

   Once again, the visioning process – doing it in your mind's eye – is very effective. Without spending money or a lot of time, you can picture or model the way something will work, and how it will be made. This is also why tools such as CAD (Computer Assisted Design) and virtual reality were created. These give us a computerized image of what, up to now, we have only been able to see in our mind's eye.

5. *Open your mind.*
   Vision is not just logical thinking. It requires creativity. Therefore, you need to open your mind to new ideas. If you are logic-oriented, you should try to be receptive to the creative imagery of your right brain. If you're artistic, you will need the more rational, linear thinking of the left brain.

   Do not try to force this. Fear and pressure block creativity. Sometimes it helps to listen to music. Taking a short walk or doing some breathing or relaxation exercises can also help to open your creative channels.

6. *Take the time to learn.*
Another way to open your mind is through learning. Talk to people in your industry. Look at what others are doing. Look for new developments and trends. Go to trade shows and read magazines, not just on your own field but on related areas. Or other areas that interest you. Your creative side will see connections that your linear-logical side might overlook.

A good example of this is the multimedia and electronics field. The telephone, computer, TV, and fax are separate pieces of equipment. But the vision of "connectivity" led us to put them together. Computers with fax/voice capability. Telephone companies providing Internet services. Computers playing music and video CD-ROMs. The possibilities now seem endless.

7. *Change perspective.*
Find ways to look at things differently. Think about alternative futures for your industry in the next twenty years. Imagine how you could make your product in a totally different way. Consider how to provide your service to an entirely new group of customers.

Changing how you see things will change how you do things.

There were two men who sawed wood for a living. One focused on his task, the other on his tools.

Both began their craft in the age of the long, straight metal saw. It was made of shiny, tempered steel, with big sharp teeth. The feel of it sawing through wood was like putting a knife through butter.

When power saws were introduced, the man who focused on his task took naturally to them. He enjoyed the ability to cut more wood, faster. But the one who took pride in his tools was perplexed. This spinning blade did not look right. There was too much power, and it made him afraid that he might cut himself.

When the laser saw was introduced, the first man was overjoyed. He'd never been able to cut so much wood so easily and precisely. He increased his production 200-fold by nightfall.

That same day, the second man retired. He could not imagine himself working without his trusty saws — and cutting wood with a beam of light.

8. *Associate with the right people.*

Do you have an optimistic or pessimistic vision? Do you love or hate your work? Do you focus on your task or on your tools? This often depends on whom you associate with.

Most of us see things the way our friends do. That's why we hang out together. However, their *attitudes* could be affecting our *altitude*. In other words, the visions of others influence how high we fly and how far we go.

We become like the people we associate with – so choose your friends carefully!

How Do We Experience Vision?

Vision comes to us on "all channels." Through all our senses. We are influenced by sights, sounds, smells, touch, and taste. Internally, we have similar senses. We also experience "knowing," a combination of thought and feeling. Our visions, dreams, and imagination are triggered by all of these sensations.

Different people experience vision differently. Those who are visually oriented see images. Those who are auditory will tend to hear words and sounds within. And those who are kinesthetic will feel what their future could be like.

It can create conflict

Think about the visions you have, the goals you want to reach. Now look at where you are. If your vision is great, the distance between *where you are now* and *where you want to be* will also be great. That creates conflict within us. We might think:

"Is it possible? Are we crazy? How will we ever get there?"

Imagine Leonardo da Vinci, sketching pictures of "flying machines" — 500 years before man would actually fly in an airplane.

Or Robert Fulton, inventor-to-be of the steam engine, being told by the great Napoleon, "You would make a ship sail against the wind and currents by lighting a bonfire under her decks? I pray you excuse me. I have no time for such nonsense."

This conflict between vision and our current reality can be hard to reconcile. There is a struggle within us to choose — or give up — one or the other.

But leadership is about accepting *both*. "Keeping our feet on the ground and our eyes on the stars," as Theodore Roosevelt put it. Being both practical and idealistic. Accepting our current reality, yet still being committed to our vision.

This acceptance of apparent opposites is called a paradox. It is important to accept both sides of the paradox because both are true. We are here now. But we create new realities through our vision.

During the early days of World War II, England was, in the eyes of the rest of the world, in its darkest hour. Belgium had surrendered to the Nazis, France had fallen, Russia had apparently aligned with Hitler, and the United States was not yet involved in the war.

When Germany seemed about to launch its long-threatened invasion of Great Britain, Winston Churchill shared his vision with his fellow countrymen:

> We shall defend our island, whatever the cost may be. We shall fight on the beaches. We shall fight on the landing grounds. We shall fight on the fields and in the streets. We shall fight in the hills. We shall never surrender.
>
> Let us brace ourselves to do our duties, and so bear ourselves that, if the British Empire and Commonwealth last for a thousand years, men will say, "This was their finest hour."

His vision helped a battered British military keep fighting until Russia and the United States had time to organize enough resources and personnel to turn the tide of the war. The creative genius of Churchill's statesmanship lay in his

ability to envision the result he wanted in its fullest expression, and then to
hold fast to his vision while remaining in touch with current reality.

What Blocks Vision?

Here is a list of some common blocks. If you experience any of them,
do not be alarmed. Just be *aware*. First you have to notice them. Then
you can do something about them.

Pressure and too much to do.

Our minds are continually being pushed and pulled. Filled from the outside. Distracted at work by meetings, memos, phone calls, and the Web, and
at home by TV, videos, magazines, and talk talk, talk talk, talk talk talk . . .

Vision needs space. A moment in the madness. Time to be still, to
think . . . and to reflect. Too much activity and pressure closes the mind.

Failure to believe in ourselves.

When we de-value our own ideas and doubt we have the power to make
them real, how can we expect others to share our vision?

Remember: You can't sell an idea to someone else if you haven't first
sold it to yourself. Start by selling yourself to yourself!

Fear.

Many of us are afraid to dream because we have been hurt before or our
dreams have not come true. It seems safer and less painful to not look
at what we want than it does to have a vision.

Here is another paradox. Our past vision may not have been successful.
Yet it is only by having more vision that we will get out of where we are now.

Lack of awareness and forgetfulness.

Often we are not aware of the visions we have. Having put them aside for so long, we don't realize that's what they are. It's like when we awaken in the morning and so quickly forget our dreams of the night before. But visions are "dreams" you don't want to forget! If you want to remember your visions, you must write them down.

Failure to choose.
We are pulled in many different directions by the "shoulds and wants" inside us. As a result, we do not focus on accomplishing one vision at a time. The visions continue to come. But they remain as ideas and do not get turned into results.

Imbalance.
Whole brain vision must combine logic *and* intuition. Heart and head. Thought and feeling. If you are too focused on one, you will lose the other.

TIPS TO DEVELOP YOUR VISION
- Decide on what you want/your goal.
- Write down your ideas.
- Get a clear picture — what does it look, sound, feel like?
- Replay your vision — visualize or picture it while lying in bed or waiting for appointments.
- Dream your vision — before you go to bed, tell yourself you want to "see it in your dreams."
- Find examples of others who have had successful visions and learn from them.
- Act on your vision — and build on each little success.

Make your living
doing what you love;
ethically, passionately, and
never give up.
– JERRY GOODIS, CANADIAN MARKETING GURU

The vision always precedes reality.
– TOM LEON, PRESIDENT, LEON'S FURNITURE

LEADING WITH PASSION

Most people know what to do,
but they don't do what they know —
because they haven't found their inner drive.
Their passion.

— TONY ROBBINS

Ask yourself these questions:

- What do I love to do?
- What do I feel strongly about deep within?
- What moves or inspires me?
- Is there something I love to do or share, even if I do not get paid for it?

These are some of the signs of passion.

WHAT IS PASSION?

Earlier I said that vision is the idea that leads us forward. Passion, then, is what drives us. It is the energy that turns vision into action.

Passion can be described in many ways. Love. Motivation. Inspiration.

Caring. But few words can really capture it. That's because passion is a *feeling*.

In our culture, we are obsessed by words. Reading, writing, and talking. These come from our intellectual or thinking side. But there is another side to us. It is our emotional or feeling side.

Men were once taught to develop their thinking side first. That's one reason why you used to see more men as engineers, lawyers, accountants, broadcasters, and politicians.

Women, on the other hand, were raised to honour their feelings. Mothers were the nurturers of the household. Girls were given more permission to express their emotions. Still today, when women get together, they share their feelings. In public positions, women are more likely to express compassion and caring. (Women create rapport. Men create reports.)

Despite these differences, everyone has both sides. Thoughts and feelings. Vision and passion. It is the acceptance, and expression, of both sides that makes a leader-from-within.

Feelings are simple

Feelings are simple things. So, too, are passions. Love. Hate. Wanting to get. Wanting to give. The desire to do, to go, or to win.

What complicates them are our thoughts. *What* we want. *Where* we want to go. *Who* we want to be with. *When* we are going to act. It is deciding between all these different thoughts that complicates our lives.

That is why it's so important to clarify your vision. It gives you the answer to the "who, what, when, where" questions of life, and insight into what will bring you fulfillment.

If the vision is clear, the passion comes.

Passion has power

One of the ways I learned about the power of passion is through my running.

Some years go, I began to run in order to lose weight. Eventually I joined a running club that was based at the Fitness Institute in Toronto.

A number of people in the club ran marathons. When I first met them, I thought they were crazy. It was one of the most ludicrous ideas I had ever heard. Yet, within nine months, I had decided to become a marathon runner myself. Since then, I have completed nineteen of them.

If someone had tried to get me to run twenty-six miles before this, I would have laughed at them. They *could not have forced me*. (Even if they had, I probably would have collapsed.) The difference was that now I was motivated to do it. With that came the courage and the willingness to train so I could accomplish my goal.

When the motivation comes from within, you will and can do almost anything. Through this experience, I learned that passion is stronger than force, and desire is more powerful than willpower.

> *It's not the size of the army but the power within the army.*
> — NAPOLEON BONAPARTE

Many of us were taught to de-value our feelings. To discount them — if not to ignore them outright. But this is a mistake. If you don't think feelings are important, look at advertising.

Words may tell us what, where, and how much. But Madison Avenue knows it is feelings that make us buy.

What feelings? Safety, security, success. Feeling loved and feeling good. Power, excitement. Tranquillity, satisfaction, or pure joy.

Instead of channel-surfing the next time you have the TV on, watch the commercials. Hear the words. Listen to the music they play. Watch the pictures. Then see how you feel. Try the same thing with TV shows that attract you (or repulse you!). You will learn more about your feelings than any book could ever teach you.

> *Ideas, facts, and figures may inform the world.*
> *But emotion moves it.*

E-MOTION AND ENERGY

"E-motion" is energy in motion. It's a current. A flow. But it is like electricity. Unless you plug into it, it will not do anything for you.

The leader-from-within plugs into this energy. The inner flow of caring and love. The desire to express and create. The passion to excel, learn, and grow.

Think about an actor. Picture someone who knows all his lines by heart – but who has no vitality. What would you call him . . . dead, limp, or boring? Now think about one who has energy. Each word, each motion speaks of it. There's an electricity. A magnetism. A power, presence, and passion.

It is important not to confuse this energy with busy-ness. Everyone has experienced hectic days. Days when you seem to be running from one thing to another, but without much satisfaction. At the end of the day, you feel drained. This is the energy that drives the leader-from-without. It is action under duress. Struggle. You feel like fighting or resisting, and you'd rather not do it again.

Passion is just the opposite. It is a drive that refuels and restores. It increases enthusiasm. You may feel tired at the end of the day, but you have a smile on your face. And you look forward to tomorrow so you can do it again.

> *When you find your passion or your drive, it's like you're not doing it to be successful or to make some money. You love all those additional things that happen. But you're doing it because that's what you love.*
>
> *It gets you up early and it keeps you up late. You notice things. You have an impact and you have a sense of contribution. And life is really joyous.*
>
> – TONY ROBBINS

Energy must be used

One of the things most people do not realize about energy is that *we must use it to have it*. This principle applies to many aspects of our lives.

For example:

> *Learning*: The energy you invest (e.g., in reading, seminars, and lectures) determines what you will get out.

> *Exercise*: If you are tired, often the best way to get more energy is to spend some. Get up, move, and exercise!

> *Friendship*: The best way to have friends is to be a friend.

> *Money*: If you want to be truly rich, you have to *feel* rich. To feel rich, you need to give and spend. Money is only powerful when it circulates.

With energy, the general guideline is: *What you put out, you get back.* If you have passion as a manager, the people around you will have passion. (And you will get more in return.) This is also true for other types of energy and emotion. If you withhold your excitement, or create fear in others, you will get the same back from them.

Once again, that's why it is so important to decide what you want to experience. You can then choose the attitudes and behaviour that will create those results.

Do the right thing

> *It is more important to do the right thing than to do the thing right.*
> — PETER F. DRUCKER

Doing "the right thing" springs from passion. It is a commitment that honours our values and expresses what we believe in.

Often, this is not easy. Many of us would rather play it safe than say or do what we feel is right. However, following the integrity of our conscience brings satisfaction and a greater sense of peace within.

In doing "the thing right," we are often acting out of fear. We are driven by the need to be perfect or to be accepted by others. This is a characteristic of the leader-from-without. It goes back to trying to please our parents, our God, our teachers, and our boss. It creates a lot of judgement of ourselves and others, and results in a lack of personal fulfillment.

> The stronger your feelings are for what you do
> — and the more you believe you are doing the right thing —
> the greater your passion will be.

People May Think You Are Crazy

Very few people live with passion and vision. That's why those who do appear to be crazy. It's so different from what most people are used to.

Elvis. The Beatles. Columbus. The Wright brothers. Laura Secord. Edison. Walt Disney. Roberta Bondar. Modern-day management experts like Tom Peters, Peter Senge, and Henry Mintzberg. All of them were told they were crazy or that what they wanted to do was impossible. (These comments about pioneers and new ideas are made so often, they may even be a sign that you are going in the right direction!)

Personally, I believe that people should follow their hearts even if it seems crazy. As long as it is not going to kill you or others, do what you believe in. Try what seems impossible. Devote yourself wholeheartedly to your vision.

By giving your all to it, you will have a better chance of accomplishing it.

"When I discovered what synchronized swimming was all about, I was seven years old. I thought it looked like fun so I wanted to learn. When I started, I never really thought about going to the Olympics or being the world champion. All I knew is that I loved it. I wanted to learn more about it. I couldn't wait to go back the next day. Nothing could make me miss one single day of training!

Now when I look back at my career, I realize what my sport is to me. Synchro is my life, my dream. Synchronized swimming is a passion for me. And representing my country at the Olympics, swimming in front of the whole world with my heart and my soul, was the most intense and precious moment of my life!!

I believe that when you have a passion or a dream in your life, nothing can stop you or even slow you down. It becomes the fuel of your life, the sunshine in your day. It also makes you discover all the energy and the power that you have within yourself!!! It is without any doubt the best thing that can happen to someone in their life: discovering their PASSION."

— SYLVIE FRECHETTE
GOLD MEDAL WINNER, 1992 OLYMPICS

Olympic champions are almost always called crazy at some time in their lives (*before* they win). Think about it. They see clearly what they want: to be the best in the world. They work their butts off — getting up early and training long hours. The rest of the world says they are nuts and wonders why they don't slow down and enjoy life.

But they *are* enjoying life. Being the very best is their vision, their mission. It is one of the greatest motivations anyone can have, and they are prepared to give their all to achieve it.

That's passion.

The next time someone tells you "It can't be done," remember these predictions:

Everything that can be invented has been invented.
— CHARLES H. DUELL, COMMISSIONER,
U.S. OFFICE OF PATENTS, 1899

This "telephone" has too many shortcomings to be seriously considered as a means of communication. The device is inherently of no value to us.
— WESTERN UNION INTERNAL MEMO, 1876

We don't like their sound, and guitar music is on the way out.
— DECCA RECORDING CO.,
REJECTING THE BEATLES, 1962

DOES EVERYBODY HAVE PASSION?

I believe we start out that way. As kids, most of us have a passion for life. We love exploring, learning, and trying new things. We also have great vision of what we can be and do. But as we grow older, many of us lose it. This may be the greatest loss we will ever experience.

Parents and teachers may find it difficult to deal with our energy. They tell us not to act out or be different. Sometimes we are told we will never amount to anything. People may laugh at our visions and passions.

We also get discouraged when we are not successful or do not achieve what others have said we "should." We experience a sense of failure. We may even conclude that dreams are not possible. Why have passion when it doesn't get us anywhere?

I have also observed that many people do not see the good they have done in life. Consider Jimmy Stewart's character, George Bailey, in the movie *It's a Wonderful Life*. Instead of travelling and seeing the world, he has to remain in his small home town. He helps dozens of families build houses, grow happy families, and create a prosperous, safe community. But he almost throws it all away – because he feels his life has been worthless. (If you haven't seen the movie, rent it – or watch for it on TV around Christmas time.)

When you see life this way, it saps your energy, your drive, and your belief in yourself.

PASSION NEEDS REPLENISHING

Passion is always in us. But it may be buried or dormant. It is like an untapped reservoir of water, far below the surface. To flow, it must be tapped and brought to the surface.

You can tap that reservoir inside by "replaying the good stuff." Think about times in your life when you have made a difference, been successful, or helped others. Remember how you felt. Think of when you first started living with your mate. When you moved to a new home or apartment. When you bought your first car, stereo, or computer. How do you feel about these events now?

The feelings of passion and vitality diminish over time. When we take something for granted, we lose sight of its value. We forget to see the good we have done and the wonder of all that is around us.

There are so many reasons to feel fulfilled. Look around you. At your home, family, business, and community. No matter where you live in Canada, it is extremely safe and secure. You can work and accumulate money or wisdom, as much as you want. But you may not appreciate it fully.

It is crucial that we appreciate and enjoy what we have. Leaders-from-within do this far more than leaders-from-without. This gives them more good feelings — and they create more as a result.

Look around the room. Everything you see was somebody's vision at one time. It is awesome to consider . . .

Want to rekindle your passion? Start by remembering your vision — what it is you are trying to build or grow. The clearer it is, the more intense your feelings will be. Conversely, you will lose energy when you forget where you are going.

It all goes back to knowing yourself. What is your purpose or your goal? What are you working towards? As you reclaim your vision, you will reclaim your passion.

Religion is good for this. It gives people a distant end goal and a high purpose: Being with the Almighty. Social and environmental goals are also valuable. Working for something greater than ourselves lights the fire within. Find something that makes your fire burn brightly.

Why Is Passion Important?

- *It is the energy that moves people from within.*
  It comes in different forms:

  - inspiration
  - desire

- drive
- devotion and caring

In our culture, we are shifting away from authoritarian leadership; that is, leadership by rules, force, and controls. People don't want that any more. But we need to find something to replace it. Vision and passion help us do that. They move us from within.

By leading yourself this way, you are then able to lead others – by creating an environment where authority and leadership come from inside them.

- *Passion brings vitality.*

    Do you work to survive, or do you work to thrive?
    After "earning a living" today, will you have more life?

Vitality is the energy of life. It is the "living" we are all working to earn. The juice that perks up relationships. The spirit that makes an organization dynamic or a community healthy.

Vitality improves our circulation and breathing. It makes our heart stronger and improves our sex life. It brings light to our eyes and life to our step.

Think of what it's like to *work* until 2 a.m. Now think of what it's like to dance, play sports, or do your hobby until that hour. In which do you have more passion? In which do you have more life?

- *Making your vision real depends on it.*
  Vision without passion is just an idea. Passion is doing what you love – and loving what you have to do to get there.

- *It keeps you going and brings commitment.*
  Passion motivates you to act and to keep moving towards your goals. It brings a level of commitment far beyond anything your will or external force can match.

- *It makes you more effective.*
  Passion draws up all the energy and talents you have. You become so committed, so wholehearted in your desire, that you spare nothing to reach your goal. The phrase "give it everything you've got" is really a call for passion.

- *Passion brings up other positive emotions.*
  When you love to do something, that "love" brings up other positive feelings: hope, faith, expectancy, curiosity, trust, and meaning, to name a few. When you feel better, you create better results. Passion and love build on each other, just as fear, lethargy, and negativity do — in the opposite direction.

- *It takes us past "nos" and rejections.*
  The word "dispirited" means to lose energy or hope. This often happens when we are rejected or do not succeed.
  Passion and vision work together. They remind us of what's possible. They increase our faith, lift our spirits, and move us past our obstacles.

- *It helps turn "impossibles" into reality.*
  Even when ideas seem impossible, when there is passion behind them they will often be accomplished.

- *Passion is its own reward.*
  Passion brings a feeling of "resource-fullness" and a desire to give. These in turn bring satisfaction, which is the true end goal of any project. As a result, we can release some of our fears about creating results. That makes us more flexible and open, which in turn improves whatever results we want to create.

THE THREE SOURCES OF PASSION

I have found that there are at least three sources of passion. These come to us through:

1. Inheritance (you are born with or into it)
2. Doing what you love to do
3. Loving what you do.

Let me explain.

Mark Cullen is a gardener. He grew up in a family gardening business. So it is in his genes (or on his jeans – whichever).

Anyway, Mark has inherited a passion for anything that's green. He grows plants. He researches them. He talks and writes about them and has published several books. He does a weekly gardening show on radio stations across Canada. That's what has made his company, Weall and Cullen, one of Canada's outstanding garden and plant stores.

Mac Voisin is a good example of the second type of passion: Doing what you love to do. Mac was a successful home builder in the Kitchener area of southern Ontario. But his real passion was food. After some years in the building industry, he decided to open – in partnership with his brother-in-law – the first M&M Meat Shop. M&M went on to become a large franchise operation with hundreds of stores across Canada.

The third passion can be described in this way: "Wherever you are now, create a passion for what you do."

Take Mel Lastman. He used to sell furniture and appliances and created the highly successful Bad Boy stores. He moved on to become mayor of North York, Ontario, and grew it to become a major commercial and office centre rivalling downtown Toronto. He has served North York with great success for over twenty-five years. Whatever Mel does, he gets excited about it.

Look for people with passion. Observe or ask what kind of passion they have. Then look inside yourself. What kind of passion do you have?

THE TWO SIDES OF PASSION

With her passion to help others help themselves, Mary Kay Ash has brightened the lives of thousands and become one of the most influential and respected personalities in philanthropic and business circles.

"I had spent years in the sales field and when I retired," says Mary Kay, "I sat down and outlined the changes I felt would make a better company — one that would be based on the Golden Rule. I wanted to provide an open-ended opportunity to women, to help them achieve anything they were smart enough to do."

What began in 1963 as a tiny storefront operation with nine saleswomen became, as of 1995, the largest direct seller of skin-care products and cosmetics in the United States and Canada. With more than $1.5 billion in annual retail sales to nearly 23 million customers, the company had grown to more than 375,000 [sales] consultants. According to the company literature, 3% of American women earn more than $100,000 annually — and 80% of these are associated with Mary Kay.

"I believe in praise and encouragement," she says. "Nothing works better to motivate people than to have someone treat them like equals, display interest in them as human beings, and praise them for a job well done. An ounce of praise can bring remarkable results."

Sources: *The Saturday Evening Post, October, 1981*; *Contemporary Authors*; *1995 Current Biography Yearbook*

The Mary Kay story is an unusual one in business. She's highly successful. She's studied at the Harvard Business School. But many people still cannot figure out the key to her success.

I'd like to suggest an explanation. Maybe there are two sides of passion. Let's call them head passion and heart passion.

Many of us, particularly males, are used to head passion. It begins with ideas. We get a vision, like creating a new sports centre or starting a new chain of stores. We are fuelled by the thought of how big or successful it can become and we feel the desire to create it.

Mary Kay is an example of heart passion. Her success started with feelings, like caring and respect. She had a desire to help her sales consultants feel worthy and valued, and for them to pass that same feeling on to their customers.

> *Your role is not to sell cosmetics. [It is to ask yourself]* "What can I do to send these women home feeling more beautiful on the outside, knowing full well that they'll become more beautiful on the inside as a result?*

> – HER ADVICE TO MARY KAY CONSULTANTS

My role is to help women realize how fantastic they are.

— MARY KAY ASH

Mary Kay did not have a vision to create a billion-dollar organization. It was her desire to help others that paved the way to her success.

She's an excellent role model for women, and men, who want to put more heart into business.

How Do You Find Passion?

1. *Be aware of your feelings.*
   To find your passion, first be aware of your feelings — that you love or care about.

2. *Be aware of your vision.*
   Look at what you want to create. Where you want to go. What you feel inspired to do. When you uncover your vision, you also uncover your passion.

3. *Find what you give yourself "wholeheartedly" to.*
   Do you polish your car once a week, even if it doesn't need it? Do you love taking care of babies or children? Do you take care of your company as if it were your child? Do you love to talk to people, help them, or share ideas?
   Whatever you give yourself to without reservation, that is one of your passions.

4. *Listen for the words you use.*
   Words give away the secrets of the soul.
   When you use words like "love," "enjoy," "easy," "care about," and "great," you are probably getting close to your passions. Listen for them. When you hear yourself say them, check your feelings. (That's that sensation stirring in your body somewhere below your neck.)
   When you say "I don't care," "I don't love," "I have no

energy," look at why not. Something may be cutting off your feelings. If you cannot find them, it just means they have gone underground. (That's where "depression" comes from. It is a feeling that has been depressed, or not allowed to come out.)

What if you don't feel it?

If you do not feel a passion for anything, you need help! (Just joking . . .)

Actually, don't worry about it. You do not have to suddenly become something or somebody you are not. Finding passion is about unblocking who and what you already are.

Remember what I said earlier. Passion is feeling, and most of us were taught to bury or get rid of our feelings. We learned that at home, at school, and in business. So if you have no passion now, it means you have been a successful student! That's the good news.

The bad news is you now have to change courses. Today, "Feeling 101" is mandatory. But you do not get it in university. Your schoolroom is life.

Begin to watch your feelings and those of others. Look at the politicians on TV as they rant and rave at each other. Check out the top producers in your company, to see if they show passion for what they do. Watch lovers on the street, in the movies, and on TV. The more you observe, the more you will feel. The more you feel, the more you will learn about the passion within you.

Look at different personality types

Another way to learn about passion is by observing people with different personality types. The level of passion depends on the person; it doesn't matter what type they are. What does change is their way of expressing it.

An analytical person loves to think. This may be an accountant who loves to figure out ways to save money. It could be a scientist who thinks night and day about coming up with a new medical cure.

Expressive people, on the other hand, love to talk, and talk, and talk . . . They could be salespeople, entertainers, radio personalities, or seminar leaders.

The driver's passion is to move ahead. It does not matter where – just ahead. To increase sales, profits, and production. To do the same work in half the time.

Finally, amiables just care about others. They love people and animals. They make friends with their plants. Loving is their passion.

Different cultures also exhibit passion in different ways. Consider Scandinavians vs. Italians, or northern Europeans vs. southern Europeans. Northerners tend to be more reserved, serious, and limited in their expression of feelings – and therefore in their passion. Southerners are more passionate – about everything! Wine. Romance. Opera. Food. Politics. You name it.

Check out the culture of your parents and grandparents. Maybe you come from a long line of passion-depressing ancestors. If so, you will need to work a little harder at expressing yours!

WHAT BLOCKS PASSION?

We think too much and disregard our feelings.
Thinking is a useful tool. But it only uses one part of you. This is like cutting off your left arm because you are right-handed. You need both in order to be whole and effective.

We cut off feelings in many ways:

1. *Preoccupation.*
   When you are preoccupied, you are probably thinking about the past or the future. This stops you from being spontaneous and open to how you are feeling at the moment.

2. *Too many wants or goals. Too much pressure.*
   By trying to go too fast in too many directions, you get scattered. You feel drained. Overloaded. Tired. These feelings are signs to slow down and focus. Create some space and ask yourself what

you really want. Make some clear choices — then let the rest go
for now.

3. *Fear.*

   Fear is rampant in our society. We are afraid to lose our jobs.
   Afraid of crime and the state of our environment. We are also
   afraid to take risks, to fail, or to speak out. Fear blocks our
   feelings about doing and saying what comes naturally.

   I know things seem serious. But lighten up a little. You will
   let a more positive passion through and be more effective in creating results.

4. *Obsession.*

   Passion and focus are strengths. But when they go overboard,
   they can turn into obsession. This is being so focused on one
   thing that you lose perspective. You disregard your feelings and
   other people. You become so attached to what you want that
   you cannot find peace or enjoyment in the rest of life. This is
   how addictions to work, food, sex, money, etc., develop.

We fail to see our successes, accomplishments, and value.
Remember that you build on past success. If you feel successful, you will
become more successful. If you see your abilities, you can use them to
become stronger.

When you focus only on failure or the negative, this is how you will
feel. Any passion you have will be blocked, or turned into anger and
frustration.

We do not accept ourselves.
If you have learned that it is not okay to be emotional or enthusiastic, you
will not have passion. It's as simple as that. (By the way, if you think it's
not "cool" to be enthusiastic, look at any sports team after a major victory.)

We are afraid of where passion will take us.
It's like riding a horse for the first time. Many of us have a fear that it
will take off and we won't be able to control it.

Passion needs freedom. To move, to run, to jump. It also needs rein. If you do not have both, either your emotions will be out of control, or they will be so controlled that you will feel no life in them.

If your tendency is to resist your passion, take some time and reflect. What's the worst that could happen? Where could you let go a little? Where do you want to keep control?

Passion in Your Organization

Were you as miserable when you were hired –
or did you get like that working here?
— SIGN SEEN ON AN OFFICE WALL

Here are three signs to know if there is passion in your company, organization, or department:

1. Are people happy about what they do?
2. Do they work hard without being pushed?
3. Are people excited about their work?

If you are a leader, here's a tip. Your success will not come primarily from managing resources and equipment. It will come from maximizing the positive *energy* in people. Passion. Enthusiasm. Synergy. Well-being and satisfaction. This idea applies to your customers, staff, partners, shareholders, and suppliers. Positive energy will create positive results.

Try it with your company, association, your family – and yourself.

Tips to Find More Passion

- Give yourself permission to let your feelings out more often.
- Focus – do not try to do too many things.
- Give yourself wholeheartedly to some project or relationship.
- Lighten up – don't take yourself/your work quite so seriously (at the end, you will die anyway . . .)

- Question yourself — ask yourself "how do I feel?" not just "what do I think?"
- Listen to language — do you hear feeling words or thinking words when you or others speak?
- Work with passion — inject inspiration, enthusiasm, devotion, and caring into your work.
- Associate with others who have passion — it's contagious.
- Replay good news to build on good feelings; the more you replay good news, the better you feel.
- Laugh long, laugh often; not at others, but at life.

You cannot kindle a fire in any other heart until it is burning in your own.

— RALPH WALDO EMERSON

Taking Action

Review What You've Learned . . .

$$\textbf{A}\text{ttitudes} + \textbf{B}\text{ehaviour} \Rightarrow \textbf{R}\text{esults}$$

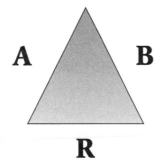

Attitudes

- Get clear on your vision. Feel your passions.
- Get clear on the results you want to create.
- See and go beyond what is known or currently possible. At the same time, stay practical.

- The best vision combines logic and intuition. The best passion combines head and heart. Both require thinking and feeling.
- Don't let the fear of being "different" stop you.

Behaviour

- Focus. Do not try to do too much; you may accomplish nothing.
- Associate with people who express vision and passion. Support them and be supported.
- Develop shared vision when working with others.
- Do not reject others for being different. See what you can learn from their different perspectives.

Results

- The more vision and passion you have, the better you feel. The better you feel, the better the results you create.
- Vision and passion are stronger than force and control. To improve results, find out what you/others care about. Harness that inspiration and energy.

. . . AND STRENGTHEN YOUR LEADERSHIP MUSCLES
(Exercises)

1. Ask

a) What strong ideas or visions do you have? What would you really like to do or accomplish? What do you care deeply about?

b) Questions to ask others at parties:
"What do you have a passion for?"
"What do you love to do?"

c) Do *you* have a personal/business vision or mission statement? (If not, write one.)

d) What is your good news this week? (Replay it.)

2. Act

a) Select one vision/passion to act on this week. Set a goal for what you want to accomplish.

b) Express your vision to others. See how it feels to share it. Refine it as you go.

c) Be passionate about something today. Find something you care about and give it your all. Share that energy with others.

3. Associate

a) Look for three people who have vision and passion.

b) Watch them. Study them. Spend time with them.

Worse than being blind is to see and have no vision.
— HELEN KELLER

TAKE RISKS

Leading with Courage

I do not guarantee you fulfillment and
happiness if you take risks.
But if you want fulfillment and happiness,
you will have to take risks.
— Peter Urs Bender

Vision shows us how the future could be. Passion moves us to create it. The risk lies in taking action to make our vision a reality.

Suppose you have a dream to start your own business. A desire to create a cure for cancer. A longing to become an artist or a dancer. Great! But if you do not act on it, your dreams will remain unfulfilled.

> *Often the difference between a successful [person] and a failure is not one's better abilities or ideas, but the courage that one has to bet on one's ideas, to take a calculated risk — and to act.*
> — Maxwell Maltz

Risk involves change and uncertainty, and with those often comes fear. That's the bad news.

The good news is: *You do not have to be perfect.* You *will* make mistakes. You cannot possibly know the "right" way to do what you have never done. What is important is that you *try*.

Is Risk What You Think It Is?

Many people see me as a risk-taker. For example, I came to Canada at the age of twenty-three without a job or a knowledge of English. Later in my career, I became a professional speaker, even though at the beginning I had a great fear of public speaking. I have flown gliders, skydived, paraglided and . . . well, let's just say I have taken a few "risks." Yet I do not really see *myself* as a risk-taker.

At first that puzzled me. But I looked at other leaders, including those who responded to my survey for this book. Many of them also ranked risk-taking fairly low. Then it hit me:

From the "outside," many activities look like risks. But from the "inside," they are not.

Most successful individuals I know take action *because they want to fulfill their vision*. That is what makes them successful.

When I came to Canada in 1967, I had a clear vision: to advance my career. In Switzerland, you have to know three languages to make it to the top in the business world. I knew only Swiss-German. So I needed to learn English, and came to Canada to do that.

When I skydived in 1968, I did so for one reason: I wanted to tell my friends back home that I did it. (Not a great vision, but it got me through one jump!) When I took up public speaking, I wanted to become successful in business. When I self-published *Secrets of Power Presentations*, it took me a long time to write and cost a lot of money to print. I had no idea if I would ever get any sales or return. But I was told by other speakers that having a book was the best way to market – so I wanted that book.

In each case, I had a vision. I knew what I wanted. In order to reach it, I had to take action. This is why to me they were not risks.

That doesn't mean I wasn't afraid. I was – and it took courage to get me through. But I simply did what was necessary to fulfill my vision.

What is risk-tasking?

For me, risk-taking is pushing yourself to do something you don't feel comfortable doing, to accomplish the goal that you seek. Here are some examples:

Expressing yourself – when you are afraid of what the reaction will be. Examples of this could be asking your boss for a raise, asking someone out on a date, or speaking up in front of others.

Trying something new – when you aren't sure whether it will work or you can master it. Examples: driving a car for the first time, learning to ski, starting a new career.

Investing something you value – without knowing if you will get it back. Examples: investing money to make more money in the stock market, or risking your life to skydive.

Changing your way of living – but being afraid to give up your current lifestyle. Examples: dieting or healthy eating, stopping smoking, changing jobs or relationships, learning a new skill.

Risk-taking always involves fear. The fear of failure, loss, criticism, embarrassment, or pain. In a way, it feels as if you are putting your life on the line. Sometimes you really are. But most of the time you're risking your self-image or identity, or something else you value, like money, position, or security. (It just feels as if you could lose your whole life . . .)

Before I started my own business, I was sales manager for an American computer software company. I sold software programs to the insurance business throughout Canada and the Caribbean.

The company treated me wonderfully. I flew all over — always in business class. Everywhere I went they wanted me to use limousines, not taxis. All my expenses were paid. It was a very cushy job and it paid very well. However, they wanted me to relocate to Indianapolis and I did not want to move.

I could have joined the competition. But my long-term vision was to work for myself. So on March 2, 1987, I launched my own one-man company — The Achievement Group.

In the beginning, it was a shock. I had doubts about whether I would succeed. My income plummeted, and of course I paid my own expenses. I hardly went to the airport anymore. When I did I went in my own car, parked in el-cheapo parking lots, and flew in the back of the plane.

Yet it was the best thing I ever did. I now feel more successful than I ever felt before. I work when I want, where I want. (As long as it is twelve hours a day, six days a week . . .) And I love it.

Risk is in the mind of the beholder

Would *you* buy a company that had worldwide sales of $700 million one year, but only $300 million the next? Probably not.

Yet that is exactly what Dr. Michael Cowpland, president and CEO of Corel Corporation, did when he bought WordPerfect in 1996. Despite growing competition from Microsoft Word, he believed that, with some changes, WordPerfect would be "the world's best word processor." He took the risk to make it part of his software empire.

Some people like taking risks. Even big ones. Climbing Mount Everest. Flying to the moon. Risking all they have at Las Vegas. They do not seem to be afraid of failing.

For other people, even the smallest risk is too great. It could be saying how they feel, going to a new movie, or trying a new restaurant.

What makes the difference?

The size of the fear in your mind – compared with the vision you are seeking – determines the size of risk you are taking.

As I mentioned earlier, I was deathly afraid of flying, skydiving, and speaking in public. But my visions were so strong that they drove me past my fears. I did not even think of it as risk-taking.

Low achievers see the fear of risk and hold back.

High achievers see potential results and go for it.

Remember: Risk is in the mind of the beholder. Taking risks is not about being without fear. It is about wanting your goal so much that you are prepared to face your fear and do it anyway.

Why Is Risk-Taking Important?

It is really quite simple. All growth depends on it.

It's the way the child learns to walk. How the apprentice gets to be a master. How you move from your first cold call to being a tele-marketing specialist; or from your first speech to being a professional speaker.

As I have said before, life isn't fair. You do not get everything handed to you on a platter. Life is often uncomfortable. Yet you take risks because it is the only way you can move ahead and live your dreams, rather than just dreaming about them.

Here are just some of the benefits of taking risks.

- **It creates action.**
  Risk-taking turns ideas and feelings into action. Action produces results. Results bring you more of the feelings, experiences, and things you want.

- **You improve your results.**
  Results depend on attitudes and behaviour. If you want to improve what you are getting, you need to change what you are thinking and doing. That is a risk.

- **You get more self-esteem and hope.**
  When you face a fear, you get more confidence. Even if you fail, you know you attempted it. With confidence comes hope. When you start to think that you can accomplish new things, the vision and passion also start to flow.

- **You increase your probability of success.**
  Suppose you don't like making sales calls. However, you need to – because it's your job, or you run your own business.

  People who know the sales profession know that you cannot sell to everyone. Maybe you can sell to one person in five. Maybe one in twenty-five. (It depends on what you are selling.) But it is a reasonably low percentage.

  Say you get a sale every tenth call. If you make only nine calls, you may not get even one sale. If you make a hundred calls, you will probably get close to ten sales.

  Now for the question: Is it a risk to keep calling? It is to your ego or your leader-from-without. None of us likes to hear "no!" or to be rejected. However, if you want to create results, all you have to do is *keep making those calls*!

Henry Ford failed and went broke five times before he finally succeeded.

Richard Hooker, the author of M*A*S*H, worked on the book for seven years, only to have it rejected by twenty-one publishers before it was finally published by Morrow. It became a runaway best-seller, was turned into a hit movie, and later became a highly successful television series.

Steve Jobs and Steve Wozniak, the inventors of the personal computer that helped launch the PC revolution, were turned down by both Atari and Hewlett-Packard before they started their own company: Apple.

Many of life's failures are [those] who did not
realize how close they were to success
when they gave up.
      – AUTHOR UNKNOWN

- **By taking risks, you learn what works.**
  When Edison invented the electric light, he tested close to 10,000 different materials as filaments. The filament is the piece of wire inside the bulb. It's what heats up and begins to shine when electricity is sent through it.

  You could say he failed 9,999 times, or that he was successful once. The point is, he found out what worked.

  Was it crazy for him to have tried so many times? Yes. He gave it far more tries than most of us would have. Yet somehow he had the confidence – or he "knew" – that he would come up with the right answer. And we are all thankful that he did.

  The same is true with doing anything new. Inventing. Creating a new consumer product. Designing a computer program. Learning to lead. To find out what works, you will also need to find out what does not.

- **Risk-taking shows how far you can go.**
  It is good to push yourself. It shows how much you can do. Your capacity and potential are always greater than you think.

- **It conserves mental energy.**
  The longer you take to make a decision, the harder it is to make. Indecision is an energy drainer. So is waiting until you can "do it perfectly." A common element of leaders and successful people is that they make decisions and take action, and avoid draining their energy.

- **It gives you peace of mind.**
  Most of us regret the things we have not done more than the things we have.

Worry less. Take more chances.
— W. P. KINSELLA, AUTHOR OF *Shoeless Joe*
(MADE INTO THE MOVIE *Field of Dreams*)

Risk Means Taking Action

I've said that successful people have a clear vision that motivates them to take risks. This vision is important; but it's not enough. Success is achieved by taking consistent action. That is *essential*.

Action is what makes vision real in the world around us. It turns the inventor's dream into a useful invention. It puts bricks, steel, or cement to the architect's plans. It is the manufacturing and marketing that brings new products to the public.

So why is taking actions a risk?

Start by asking yourself that question. (Your own best answers lie within.) Are you reluctant because you might have to give up other things you want to do? You're *right*. You do have to make choices and select priorities. Are you afraid of doing the wrong thing, or of failing to reach your goal? Both of these *are* possible. Success is not guaranteed. Do you feel it takes too much effort to reach your goal? That could be true. Goals *do* take commitment and consistent effort.

Actions take decisions, energy, perseverance, and faith. Depression, uncertainty, doubt, and fear will all try to stop you from moving forward.

But let's look at it another way. Are you really happy where you are? If you don't follow that calling within, will you be happy in the future? What would it be worth to you to feel you're alive, growing, committed, and engaged? There are no rights or wrongs; it's up to you to decide what's important to you.

Most people live their lives in a land called "wanting something better." But they're afraid to travel where they'd like to go. It means leaving the past behind and charting a course for the future. But that's what every explorer, leader, and learner must do.

Make no mistake; the journey of a thousand miles may begin with a single step, but it takes millions more to reach your destination. So be clear on what you want to do. Then do it a little bit at a time.

Daily action, in a consistent direction, *will* bring you to your goal.

The cost of being perfect

Most of us were taught to take action in the following way:

> First, you study and learn. Next you try to make a "perfect" plan.
> Then you act.

The problem is, while we're trying to be "perfect" – waiting until we have all the answers and know exactly what to do – opportunities for progress are passing us by. Successful people don't wait for perfection. That is where the "risk" comes in. It's also why they have become successful.

Think about a manager who makes decisions, not out of haste, but with reason and wisdom. One who looks at the options, sees the risks, senses what is appropriate, and gives a clear "yes" or "no."

Now think about a manager who postpones decisions for days or weeks. He cannot decide, or he is waiting for more information. He wants to avoid taking risks. But his indecision jams up the works. Other people and departments are left waiting. Hundreds of co-workers and clients may be affected because this one person does not risk making a decision.

Each day in business and government, millions of hours are wasted – and millions of ideas are lost – because we fail to decide and take action. We'd rather not say what we want. We defer because we "don't have enough information." We get a good idea, but don't value it enough to act on it. Or we say we are going to do something but fail to keep our commitments.

Inaction also results from not facing problems or bad news. How much we spent. How much we lost. Or how unhappy the employees are.

Whatever the reason, the cost is far higher than we recognize.

My suggestion is to take the following attitudes to decisions:

> "If it has to be, it is up to me!"

> *"Carpe diem* – seize the day!"

The risk of inaction

We all take two types of risks: one when we do something, and one when we do not.

That's right. We take risks even when we do nothing. In fact, inaction may be the greater of the two risks.

When you decide and act, you face situations head-on. This increases your courage and readiness. It improves clarity of thinking and focus. You may also be saving time and effort later, because you are addressing the situation before it becomes critical.

When you stop making decisions, it is often out of fear of doing the wrong thing. This fear blocks your natural creativity. Your flow of ideas, and the flexibility of thinking that comes with it. All this in turn reduces your ability to make good decisions.

Next time you are faced with a decision you'd rather postpone, make it instead. Do something; watch what happens; learn from it. Make changes based on what you learn. Keep improving the process. Then keep making decisions and moving towards your goal.

WHICH LEADER GUIDES THE RISKS YOU TAKE?

The leader-from-within is guided by wisdom — a deeper understanding of situations, supported by values and tempered by experience. This leader uses intuition as well as logic; ideals as well as practical realities.

By listening within, you will be clearer on what to do. Your potential for success will be higher. Your actions will be win-win, and better suited to the situations you face. You will also learn more in the process.

The leader-from-without often depends on others for the "right" answers or to make decisions. Alternatively, he or she may make snap decisions that can be extreme or one-sided, coming, for example, from a "me vs. you" or win-lose perspective. This leadership often results in frantic activity, or avoidance of action.

The inner leader combines self-knowledge, listening to others, and action. The external leader leaves one or more of these out. Sometimes it is the leader's own feelings. This can result in bulldozer-like action, which rolls over others' needs and feelings. Or it may lead to continual second-guessing, uncertainty, and questioning. In any case, it creates more conflict than it resolves.

There are several ways to know you are using the leader-from-within and going in the right direction. First:

- Be clear on your vision/objectives – short-term and long-term.
- Use the best information you have available.
- Listen to your intuition – and to other people.

If your action satisfies or fits all three, then proceed. If not, it is better to pause and get the piece you are missing.

Another guideline is to look at who is affected by your decision or action. As I said earlier, the best action benefits three parties:

- you
- others directly involved
- the whole.

By "the whole," I mean those not directly involved but still affected. This could include the families of your employees. Your community. The environment. The larger interests of your society.

Your interests are affected by everything and everyone around you. The more you contribute to their betterment, the more they will contribute to yours.

You can also find out which leader you are listening to by asking yourself how you feel. The externally directed leader feels pushed: "Do this. Go there. Do it right. Don't make a mistake." These leaders often do things because they feel they should or they have no choice.

The internally directed leader has a feeling that says, "I want to. I enjoy that. That feels right." From this sense of rightness comes peace of mind, clearer thinking, balance, sensitivity, and better decisions.

Remember: We all switch between the two types of leaders – a thousand times a day. Each decision we make is a choice about which leader to follow.

RISK-TAKERS IN HISTORY

Risk-taking and progress are like parent and child. You can't have one without the other.

Every advancement of human history required someone to take a risk. From the exploration of the seas to flights to the moon. From the invention of the wheel (think what it would be like to drive on square tires!) to the development of the computer. It was true for the founding of our country. The establishment of the United Nations and its peace-keeping forces. And the creation of social safety nets to help the unemployed, the elderly, and the sick.

Each and every step in our progress required a risk – a stepping forth into uncharted territory, an attempt at something new.

Here are some of my personal favourite examples of risk-takers in history.

Columbus
Think what it would have been like. You have three ships, all paid for by an investor (the Queen of Spain). You've told her your goal is to reach the new world and to bring her back a return on her investment (gold and treasures). But you do not know which direction to take. You have no high technology (only a compass) to guide you. And most people, including your crew, believe that you are going to fail by falling off the face of the earth. (Does any of this sound familiar to you?)
    The rest, as they say, is history.

Children
Children take no end of risks — walking, talking, climbing trees, riding bicy-cles, jumping off cliffs into water, going to school. Kids take more risks per day than any adult I know. Considering the size and number of risks they face, it does not look as if it would be an easy life. So why do kids have so much fun?

Walt Disney
He was born into a struggling midwestern farming family. When Walt announced that he wanted to "do what he loved" and become an artist, his

father disapproved. Then his first business venture failed. At twenty-one, the dreamer left for Hollywood to draw for the movies.

In Los Angeles, he and his brother Roy began a company to create cartoon shorts. Although they were almost penniless, and inexperienced in the film industry, Walt's tenacity and fighting spirit carried the company through.

Even before he had seen much success in films, Walt had another idea — of building a new kind of amusement park. For the next twenty years, he dreamed and worked on his hobby. In 1952, he announced his vision for Disneyland — a fantasyland for families, complete with a castle, rides of tomorrow, and mechanical animals.

Most thought he was crazy. Roy considered the concept another one of "Walt's screwy ideas" and only invested $10,000 of the Disney studio money in the project. But Walt persisted. He borrowed heavily against his life insurance policy. He convinced ABC, one of the fledgling companies in the new television industry, to become a major investor. And Disneyland opened in 1955.

Within one year, the park had gross annual revenues of $10 million and accounted for roughly one-third of overall sales at Disney.

Sources: *The Story of Walt Disney*; *Walt Disney: An American Original*

WAYS TO IMPROVE YOUR RISK-TAKING

The inability to turn dreams and wishes into results is one of our greatest shortcomings, both as individuals and organizations. I think the reason is that most of us have not learned the *skills* of taking risks.

Remember that there are two parts to risk-taking: stepping out of your "comfort zone," and taking action to reach your goal or desired outcome. Below are some tips on how to do both.

Stepping outside your comfort zone

Change is not always comfortable (except for children with dirty diapers). It takes us beyond what's familiar – our beliefs, habits, and lifestyle. Yet it's the only way we can grow and discover how much more life has to offer.

What comfort zones are you reluctant to give up? Do you resist meeting new people, eating strange foods, or wearing different clothes from what you're used to? (Some people I know are uncomfortable wearing a tuxedo — because they're not used to dressing so "fancy.") Do you feel uncomfortable changing jobs, using equipment or technology, or accepting the views of others who oppose you?

Consider these ideas to expand your comfort zone:

- *Do things you don't usually do or haven't done before.*
  Try the opposite of what you're used to doing. If making money is your big pursuit, give some of it away. If you resist setting goals, set a few and go after them.

- *Repeat an uncomfortable activity.*
  If you fear doing something — especially if it's important to your advancement (such as speaking publicly was for me) — do it *as many times as it takes* for you to feel comfortable.

- *Make choices.*
  Are you reluctant to make decisions? First, start with the small stuff: Where you want to go for lunch. What colour outfit or suit you are going to wear today. Then graduate to bigger things. What new service do you want to offer clients? How will you communicate it to them? What do you need to do to make it useful?

  Sure, you risk being wrong or having to give up something else you want; but look at the risk if you do not choose: *You will get more of what you have now.*

> If we do what we have always done,
> we will get what we have always gotten.

- *Make commitments.*
  One of the best ways to become a leader is to make promises and keep them.

> Only commit to what you can do;
> and do whatever you commit to.

- *Make definite statements.*
  Think about the low-risk statements you and others make: "I'll get back to you." "Leave it with me." "Let's do lunch some time."
  Then try this as a test. For one week, make clear decisions and statements. Use definite words like *I will* or *I won't* instead of wishy-washy words like *I could, I might, I should,* or *I'd like to.* Say what you think, feel, and believe. See how it feels, and how others respond to you.

- *Act now instead of procrastinating.*
  Procrastination is a habit. So is taking action. You will get more of whatever habit you practise. Just ask yourself: While procrastination may be comfortable, am I getting the results I want?

- *Push yourself.*
  At times it helps to challenge yourself. To stretch your attitudes and behaviour to see what is possible. You won't break, but you will discover that you can do more than you ever imagined.

- *Risk not being perfect.*
  Perfection can be a defence against action. If you're waiting until you know everything, you will never act.

- *Find ways to relax.*
  When you are rigid in your thinking (and your body), it's difficult to step outside your comfort zone. There's too much at stake; the risk is too great.
  When you relax, you are more flexible, and more open to seeing and doing things differently.

- *Know your comfort zone — and choose it.*
  Taking risks is about what feels right for *you.* It is not about me or someone else telling you what you should do.

Use your ability to say "no" when you are not ready to take a risk. When you have been given too many things to do. When you feel someone is asking you to be immoral or unethical. Stand your ground. Respect yourself.

Having the *option* to say "no" is important, even if you do not use it often. It is called having control. Those who feel they have control have less stress and perform better.

Take action towards your goals

Every action takes you outside your comfort zone and a step closer to your desired result. Here are some reminders, and some new ideas, on how to help yourself take more action.

- *Remember your motivation.*
  The stronger your motivation, the more likely you will be to act. For strong motivation, you need both vision *and* passion; a dream *and* the intense feeling that you want to accomplish it.

- *Look clearly at where you are now.*
  We often don't take action because we deny what's happening around us. "Hey, we're fine financially . . ." when the debt is mounting. "There's no problem . . ." when your staff are getting ready to mutiny. "I don't really have an eating or drinking problem . . ." when everyone around you knows the truth.

  By looking clearly at where you are now and accepting it, you will see and feel what you need to do. Your leader-from-within already knows.

- *Decide on a direction.*
  Sometimes, you may simply not know what to do. At times like this, decide on the direction you want to go. "I want an improvement in this situation." "There must be a way to stop this fighting between us." "There must be an answer to this problem."

When the student is ready, the master appears. When your heart and mind decide what they want to accomplish, the means will follow.

- *Define your vision/goal.*
  Select a goal that gives you the most satisfaction, or feels right to you (based on your needs and wants).

  When your goals are clear and you are committed to them, you will naturally begin to do whatever is needed to accomplish them.

  > Take high-performance athletes. They know the foods, lifestyle, and training practices they need to have the highest clarity and energy. If their goal is to win, their choices are made. They don't waste time procrastinating or holding on to old habits because this doesn't create the results they want!

- *Move from thinking/planning to doing.*
  Some of us assess risks logically – "What will it cost me? What benefits will I gain?" – and then decide on the most logical steps to follow. Others trust their intuition, decide what feels right, then jump into action.

  Both ways have their benefits, and their costs. Planning can be a hidden way of procrastinating or trying to be perfect. If you tend to overplan, take a risk and do it now. The opposite is true for those who act too quickly. Take time to pause and reflect on what you're doing, whom it's affecting, and how you feel inside.

- *Focus.*
  I said earlier that you don't have unlimited resources. Risk leaving other options behind, focus on one goal, and achieve it.

- *Take one step.*
  Inaction has many sources. Sometimes we dream too much. Other times we get overloaded by all we need to do, or we get paralyzed by fear, inertia, or resistance.

The way to break through these is to take one step forward. Do something specific towards your goal. If you're thinking of travelling to Barbados, call a travel agent and find out how much it costs. If you want to be healthier, start by going out for a walk. If you have been dreaming about a new car, home, or cottage, set aside a certain amount from your next paycheque and put it in a special account.

Getting started is essential to all risk-taking and action.

- *Be persistent.*

The number one message of most great achievers is this: Follow through with what you begin and "stay with it!"

Using the examples above, one walk is an important start, but it's not enough to be healthy. You need to have a regular routine. Putting some money into a special account starts the ball rolling, but it will not buy you that car, home, or cottage. You will need to take a little from *every* paycheque.

Take the risk to persist.

Nothing in the world can take the place of persistence.
Talent will not; nothing is more common
than unsuccessful men with talent.
Genius will not; unrewarded genius is almost a proverb.
Education alone will not; the world is full of educated derelicts.
Persistence and determination alone are omnipotent.
— CALVIN COOLIDGE

- *Stay on target.*

Life is full of diversions: perfecting your vision; overstudying your situation; fighting fires and handling the details. Remember your goal, stay on target, and get where you want to go.

- *Look at your results.*

Are you getting the outcomes – the results and the feelings – that you want? Are your actions benefitting others? These are the indicators that your risks are paying off. If things are not working, risk trying something different.

- *Keep learning.*

   Learning is risk-taking. It means letting go of what you believe now, so you can see how life works from a larger perspective. Here are three tips.

   Learn from the experts. They can show you how to make the difficult look easy. This will reduce your fear of taking risks and give you the confidence to take action.

   Find one thing of value from every program you watch, every seminar you attend, and every article or book you read. Then commit yourself to applying it. (This has worked very successfully for me. It keeps me taking action and moving ahead.)

   Learn by doing. Don't keep studying, do something. Learn from it, adjust, then do it again. For some, this can be a scary way to learn; but it is very practical. It takes you through your fears, teaches you what works, and creates results at the same time.

> *Life is either a daring adventure or nothing at all.*
> *Security is mostly a superstition.*
> *It does not exist in nature.*
>
> — HELEN KELLER

WHAT BLOCKS RISK-TAKING?

Fear. Fear. Fear. Fear. Fear, fear, fear.
Fear is a negative vision of the future. It locks on to your anxious feelings and triggers memories of past fears. Fear of death. Fear of failure. Fear of loss. These block positive visions and feelings from your awareness.

I have used several techniques to overcome my fears. One is being clear about my vision. The more I see the potential benefits, the more committed I am to my vision.

The second is changing perspective. I switch from focusing on my fear to focusing on my vision.

The third technique (which I mentioned briefly in the last section) is called "doing it." I do what I am afraid of. I keep doing it and doing it until it holds no fear for me. The greater the phobia, the more I have to do it to overcome it.

I used to be incredibly afraid of flying — even as a passenger on commercial airlines. I used to shake and get nauseated just at the thought of it. I had to take about forty flights before I overcame my fear. But after that I went on to learn how to solo in a glider!

Do the thing we fear,
and the death of fear is certain.
— RALPH WALDO EMERSON

Fear of criticism.

This is one of the major blocks to risk-taking. None of us likes to be criticized, especially when we are feeling vulnerable. When we are trying something new, for example, criticism can wipe out our hope and confidence in an instant.

One way to deal with criticism is by shifting goals. Instead of wanting to be "right," make it your goal to be "successful." Then every time someone gives you feedback, you can hear it as a new idea to make you more successful.

Resistance to change.

Taking risks requires the ability to let go. To risk losing the safety of what we have or know for the greatness of what we can become. It also means releasing our attachment to our problems. Strange as it may seem, a lot of us would rather hold on to our poor results ("but I've been doing my best . . .") than try something new.

Lack of a vision or goal. Lack of desire or motivation.

We all need a reason to live; otherwise we just get by. Yet many people do just that. They either have everything to live with, but nothing to live for; or they see no hope for future improvement.

So what do you do? One option is to find a religion. (Try the one your family had, or one that appeals to you today.) It is one of the oldest, strongest, most powerful reasons to live. When times are rough, it gives hope. Direction. Answers about why you are here. Ways to be a good person. It also helps you believe in yourself – and something greater than yourself. You will find others who share your values. When you feel you are doing the right thing, you find happiness.

If you do not like religion, try something else. Do what you love to do, or love something you want to do. Join an association or a charity. Help a group working for social or environmental progress. Find a movement with a vision you can share. Have passion, work with others, and create some satisfying results.

Failure to value ourselves.

Listen to your self-talk. Do you put yourself or your ideas down? Do you stop yourself from expressing your visions, hopes, or desires? Do you always give others their way, or just go along with the status quo?

Negative inner feelings.

These are what drive us inside. Feelings of lack, burden, pressure, doubt, helplessness. They are like quicksand.

Start watching your feelings. Accept them. Then begin to shift your attitude. Smiling helps. So does an erect posture. Positive self-talk. Affirmations. Seeing your talents. Having small successes.

Always build on what you have and where you are now – whether it is a high mountain or a deep valley.

Past mistakes, failures.

When you've taken risks and failed in the past, it can be hard to try again. Yet that is what it takes.

Try "reframing," or seeing past failures from a new perspective. What did you learn from them? How will they help you improve or grow?

Only those who dare to fail greatly
can ever achieve greatly.
– ROBERT F. KENNEDY

Impatience.

At the start of a project, you will normally put in more effort than you will get out in return. (This idea was described earlier in "Maximize Your Return!") You may, for example, receive only a 20 percent return by the time you have invested 80 percent of your effort. *Do not stop there.* Trust.

Any new task takes time to yield results. Education and training. Installing a new computer system. Exercise. Gardening. Starting a new career or a new business. If you quit halfway through, you may miss the good that is just down the road.

> *Overnight success comes from luck*
> *and years of hard work.*

A Risk-Avoider's Top Ten Sayings
10) "I do not have enough information."
 9) "There are too many things I want to do. I can't decide."
 8) "I'm afraid to fail (or to dream)."
 7) "I'd rather be safe than sorry."
 6) "I'll think about it."
 5) "I hate my job, but I keep working there."
 4) "I have no choices. There's nothing I can do!"
 3) "I dream a lot about what I'd like, but I seldom get it."
 2) "I can't say (or do) that!"
 1) "I'd rather take no action than make a mistake."

Do these sound like you? If so, take charge of your life — and take a risk!

RISK IN YOUR ORGANIZATION

It does not matter where you work or what you do. You will have to take risks in order to be happy.

In your family, this could mean setting limits – on how much you spend or what your children watch on TV. It could involve reaching out to make new friends when you move into a new neighbourhood. Investing in RRSPs, stocks, or bonds. Risking saying how you feel to your spouse.

In your organization, you will face similar risks – and many others. You may have to decide what new products to come out with. Whether to invest in new ventures. How much personal time to take – for renewal, exercise, and family. Whether to stay where you are, change jobs, or start your own business.

Find a risk-taking strategy that works for you. Then test it, refine it, and keep going. Support other people – in your organization, community, and country – in their risk-taking. Create a positive risk-taking environment. The more you help others, the more their positive results will help you.

Taking Action

Review What You've Learned . . .

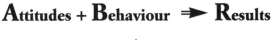

$$\text{Attitudes} + \text{Behaviour} \Rightarrow \text{Results}$$

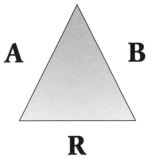

Attitudes
- You do not have to be perfect. Take the risk.
- The level of risk you face depends on your perspective. It is the difference between the size of your fear and the size of your vision.

- The leader-from-within takes risks guided by wisdom. The leader-from-without takes risks guided by fear, lack, or greed.

Behaviour

- Risk-taking means moving past our fears and towards our goals. It takes courage, a clear vision, and consistent action.
- Believe in your goal so strongly that you are willing to face what you fear and do it anyway. Keep doing it until you are no longer afraid of it.
- No one can make progress without risk. We must always leave where we are now to get to where we want to go.
- Taking no action can be a greater risk than taking action.
- Make choices and commitments.
- Find what you love to do. Take action. Be persistent.

Results

- Look at your results (material and feelings). If your risk taking is sound, your results will improve.
- Learn from your results. Risk is reduced as experience teaches you what works and what does not.

. . . And Strengthen Your Leadership Muscles
(Exercises)

1. Ask

a) Where have you been resisting taking a risk?

b) Try risk-taking at gatherings and parties. Speak to new people without being introduced. Ask people new questions, like: "What risks are you glad you have taken?"

c) Have you been underlining ideas you want to remember in this book? Is it still a "risk" to do that?

d) What positive experiences have you had with risk-taking? This week? This year? (Replay those memories!)

2. Act

    a) Pick two things you have learned from the book so far and apply them this week. (I told you I'd be testing you . . .)

    b) Take a risk each day this week. Start a project. Take some time off work. If there's something you've resisted saying to someone, say it. Spend some time with your family. Start the book you have always wanted to write.

3. Associate

    a) Identify three people who take risks.

    b) Watch them. Study them. Spend time with them. Ask what helped them to take risks.

Communicate

LEADERS AS COMMUNICATORS

Throughout history, outstanding leaders
have been ordinary people with extraordinary vision –
and the skills to communicate it.

— PETER URS BENDER

To be a leader in the years ahead, you *must* be able to communicate. How well you do it will affect your success – in life and work; in your education, associations, family, and relationships.

Please re-read the paragraph above. Once; then again; and again. This is not a *maybe*. It is a *must*. I can't emphasize that enough.

In the past, communications skills were not so consequential. But in the future, they will be an *absolute* prerequisite for success.

To me, communication is the *exchange of information and feelings* that leads to mutual understanding. Thus it is more than talking *at* each other. Communication makes a bond or a connection between giver and receiver. Between different departments. Manager and staff. Prospect/customer and salesperson. Teacher and student.

One half of communication is expression: speaking, writing, acting or performing, art. The other half is the receiving side: listening, reading, observing. Both bring ideas, feelings, and experience.

These are just our intentional ways of communicating. We also communicate unintentionally – through our attitudes, body language, voice tones, and behaviour.

Think of a speaker who bored you or excited you – was it just their words?

We communicate more than words. We communicate our energy, beliefs, feelings, and experience.

Why Is Communication So Important?

Communication is the lifeblood of today's society. It is vital to the well-being of your life and your projects, whatever those may be.

We live in an information age. Marshall McLuhan's global village has arrived. Most of our working time is spent communicating – reading, writing, talking, listening. It is a vital part of almost every job. All students use it. All companies and organizations demand it. All relationships depend on it.

Many people still take communications for granted, thinking, "I know how to talk and write. I learned that in grade school," or "It's not really important in *my* job." Do not make that mistake. You use it, and need it, much more than you think.

In today's business environment, communication is crucial in the following areas:

Sales and Marketing
- promotion and advertising
- reception, information requests, prospect follow-up
- price negotiation
- customer presentations, sales, follow-up/feedback
- consumer/market research
- bidding, requests for proposals

Service
- support and service for all products sold

Management
- internal communication of vision/mission (and passion!)
- team-building
- intra/interdepartmental cooperation
- progress and annual reports
- setting and negotiation of budgets and contracts
- employee/management relations
- board and shareholder contact
- bankers and lawyers

External Relations
- public and government relations
- industry relations/trade associations
- stockholder/investor relations

Information Systems
- software/hardware provider contacts
- negotiations, purchasing, support
- computer installation and support for internal clients

Research and Development
- technical and industry research, information exchange

Plant/Production
- scheduling
- set-up, maintenance
- quality control
- worker safety

Purchasing
- contact with product and service suppliers
- product specification and quotes
- price negotiation

Training
- employee education

Personnel/Human Resources
- hiring
- staff management
- employee review
- firing/outplacement

No matter what the position – from manager to secretary, plant worker to engineer – everyone needs good written and verbal communication skills.

Today, you must continually upgrade your information and skills to stay current. You represent your company in the marketplace, attracting (or repelling) potential sales. And you need to be able to present yourself to new employers, in this age of mergers, acquisitions, downsizing, and contract/temporary employment.

If you run your own business, communication skills are even more important – because you have to handle many of the activities listed above by yourself!

But these are just some of our work-related communications. We also need personal communication skills to enhance our relationships with friends, significant others, family, banks, insurance companies, etc., and to make our lives run harmoniously.

Not everyone sees communication the way I do. In fact, a number of leaders in our survey ranked it fairly low, compared to other factors in their success. Even I do not rank it as *the* most important factor. But communication is like water. We may take it for granted. But it's what gives us life, and makes everything else flow.

Seven Ways Communication Has Changed

1. *There is more information now than ever before – and there is even more to come.*
   Need I say more?

2. *There is more spoken communication than ever before.*
   There are more cross-departmental meetings. There is more teamwork. Telemarketing. Personal contact with clients at all

levels of companies. More networking, teleconferencing, and videoconferencing. More media contact (especially TV and radio) by more people, even home business owners and leaders in volunteer organizations.

3. *There is more e-mail, Internet, and Intranet.*
For the time being, these new modes of communication are primarily "print." But we use them interactively, as if we were speaking. And voice connections are just around the corner.

4. *We are becoming less formal.*
When using the fax, e-mail, and Internet newsgroups, presentation style is less important than content. (No need for the fancy letterhead here.) When speaking, there is less "behind the podium" and more "out there in front of people." It's time to be less formal and more "yourself."

5. *We are doing more for ourselves.*
Downsizing has meant reductions in office staff. More people are working from home. This means we have to do more of our communicating – writing and speaking.

6. *We are more visual and multimedia-oriented.*
Organizations are making extensive use of desktop publishing. Speakers are using more overheads, slides, and computerized/ electronic presentations. We are moving to CD-ROMs with full sound and motion. This is what you need to remember: People learn through more than words. If you want to communicate effectively, you will need to use graphics, charts, tables, pictures . . .

7. *We want to hear about more "personal experiences."*
Look at articles in magazines and listen to speakers. It's even on the TV news. Everywhere there are more stories of personal experience. How re-engineering or free trade affected a specific company – or even one person in a particular industry. How a top business leader became successful. How a young Swiss man

came to Canada to learn English . . .

People want information about your subject. But they also want insight into what has worked for you and how your ideas could affect them personally.

Why Is Communication Essential to Leadership?

As I said in a previous chapter, leadership is about growth. It is about moving from where we are now to where we want to be. Moving through and beyond our fears. Becoming more fulfilled and helping others.

None of this will happen if you do not share your ideas and feelings with others. People will not know your vision. They will not be able to feel your passion. No one will learn from you. No one can follow you.

What's more, you will not grow. Many speakers and teachers, for example, find that when they are communicating, they learn more than their students do. In order to teach, you have to really know your subject. You learn what works and what doesn't. What sounds logical. How people react. You hear other people's ideas, and these go beyond your own. That is when the real growth begins.

Teach – and you shall learn.

Leadership also depends on listening. As Stephen Covey, author of *The Seven Habits of Highly Effective People*, says: Seek to understand the other person before trying to be understood yourself. Do not persuade another of your position. Ask. Seek. Look at it his/her way. Restate the other person's point to their complete satisfaction – before you state or argue your own position. (I know that one very well. But it is extremely tough to do!)

Why is listening so important? It is the other side of the "bridge" between people. You can talk, preach, write, paint, or act all you want. But if no one is there to receive it, a vital element is missing.

In leadership from without, which is based on a dominance model, this is not as important. "I tell (or command!) you what to do." No questions asked. End of communication.

Leadership from within, however, is about partnership. And partnership depends on communication. On finding shared values and common ground. On teamwork — or alignment of our visions and passions — to make a difference. To be a leader-from-within, you have to know how to connect with your listeners. To understand what they want, and to work together to create it.

Another essential part of partnership is trust, or a sense of confidence in and connection with another person. This is based on integrity and caring. It comes from knowing yourself and understanding the other person. It is a relationship developed through communication.

> *Nobody cares what you know*
> *until they know that you care.*
> — AUTHOR UNKNOWN

Life is not about being a solitary individual. It is about relationship. How we get along together. How we help or hurt each other. And whether we make shared progress or try to stop each other from getting ahead.

I believe there are no self-made men or women. In anyone's success, there are others involved. Sports teams need fans; the players need one another. Companies need staff, suppliers, and clients. Salespeople need clients and customers, as well as the rest of the company — production, shipping, service, and accounting — to fulfill their customers' needs. (Even the crooked stock promoters who made millions selling junk bonds needed buyers and sellers!)

WHY DO WE HAVE TROUBLE COMMUNICATING?

Good communication, like leadership, must come from within. It is rooted in knowing our values, clarifying our vision, and experiencing our passion. It comes from self-reflection, self-acceptance, and self-worth. This inner process must occur before a leader can truly express him- or herself to the outer world.

Yet many of us are not comfortable with this "inner side" of communication. As an outwardly focused culture, we seldom take time to go inside and find out what matters to us. In addition, many of us have been taught that passion or expressing what we care about or want is "selfish" or self-centred. That valuing our vision and ideas lacks "humility" and speaking honestly or directly is "arrogant" (at least it seems to cause people to blush or get uncomfortable). And that expressing our emotions is "unprofessional."

It's no wonder we have difficulty communicating. We live in a society where it is more important to be right or acceptable than to be real. Is it any wonder we have trouble finding – or being – leaders-from-within?

Fear blocks flow

Self-expression is natural. However, when we have been repressed, feel strongly about something, or are under pressure to "perform," inhibitions and fears block our natural flow. It's true for everyone. CEOs and managers. Writers and speakers. The average person saying a few words at a family celebration. Fear blocks flow.

I know this from my own experience. Painfully shy as a child, I could not say anything in public – let alone make a speech. What got me into my current work was:

- recognizing that my fears were limiting me
- having a vision of what I wanted to accomplish
- taking the risk of learning how to present.

I joined a speakers club and learned how to overcome my fears.

In my seminars on leadership, I have participants make a few short speeches. This is to help them face their fear of speaking. I want people to feel freer in front of groups, suppliers, staff, and others; and to have the courage to express their ideas, vision, and passion.

At first, many think the course is "kids' stuff." But as soon as their names are called, you can see the fear set in. Their breathing gets shallower and faster. They look tense. They shuffle slowly up to the front, heads bowed. They almost forget their own names, let alone the content of their talks.

Remember: These are grown, successful men and women. They are highly skilled at what they do. However, they are self-conscious about expressing themselves in front of large meetings, or even small groups. Most are thinking, "What will these people think of me? Will they accept what I say?"

> It does not matter what kind of car you drove to the meeting, or if you came by bus. Whether you paid $200 or $2,000 for your suit. Whether you wear a Timex or a Rolex watch. In front of a group, fear makes us all equal.

Some people experience a different problem. They have such a strong personal vision or passion that it gets in the way of listening to others, seeing life from someone else's point of view, or communicating in a language that the other person will readily understand. This driven, seemingly self-centred behaviour may result from a strong need to be right or a hidden fear of criticism.

Whatever the fear, it breaks the bond of communication.

The three greatest human fears are:

1. Speaking in front of a group
2. Dying
3. Speaking and dying in front of a group.

When Daniel was thrown into the lions' den and those ferocious lions began to come at him, he reached over and whispered something in each lion's ear. One by one, the lions tucked their tails and slunk away.

Afterwards, someone asked, "What in the world did you say to them?" Daniel replied, "I simply told them they would be expected to say a few words — after dinner."

And now for the good news . . .

Don't let these problems hold you back. The good news is that the skills of communication – just like the skills of leadership – can be learned: How to present your ideas effectively. How to negotiate. How to ask for what you want and listen effectively.

The next chapter is devoted to building these skills, especially as they relate to public speaking. For now, let me leave you with some tips to enhance your overall approach to communication.

Ways to Improve Your Communication

All of the steps I've described for leadership from within are equally important for good communications.

1. **Attitude and behaviour affect your results.**

- *Attitude.*
  This gets communicated in everything you say and everything you do. In telephone conversations and speeches. In the way you treat your staff and suppliers, and how you go about collecting the money you're owed.

  I believe in being positive and honest, in respecting the audience. Speak (and write) from "the best in you" to "the best in them."

- *Behaviour.*
  Your behaviour is most powerful when it fully reflects your attitudes. That's why actors work to "get in the mood" before performing. They align their thoughts, feelings, actions, and words to create maximum power. (Shouldn't you?)

  It is also why someone who gives mixed messages is less effective as a communicator. When you say one thing but mean another, you leave people feeling there is something wrong. They may not know what it is but they do feel it!

2. **Communication depends on knowing yourself – *and* others.**

- *What makes you tick?*
  To be a clear communicator, you need to be clear about who you are and what matters to you. Then share experiences that have been meaningful to you.

- > *When willpower and imagination have a conflict,*
  > *it's always imagination that wins.*
  > — DR. ÉMILE COUÉ

  Imagination comes from what you want to do. Will comes from what you believe you should do. When there is a conflict between them – as in the case of "I should diet" vs. "I want to eat that incredible dessert" – the dessert normally wins.

  To change that, you need to *want* that new goal. Not "dieting" . . . but being seeing yourself slimmer, and feeling yourself healthier, happier, and more powerful. Only then will your diet win out over the dessert.

  Use this same idea to be a more effective communicator. Instead of telling people what they should do, speak to their imaginations. Help them get a clear picture of what they want, and what would excite, electrify, and sustain them.

- *Think about how you – and others – like to be treated.*
  For years I have said that caring behaviour was guided by the Golden Rule (Do unto others as you would have them do unto you). But today, that's changed. The new rule is "Do unto others as *they* want to have done unto them." I've found that I am not the only one to think this way. Authors Tony Alessandra and Michael J. O'Connor have called this "The Platinum Rule."

  It only makes sense: Treat people better and they will work better.

  Do you think others want to be: Talked down to? Motivated by fear? Told something that is not true? (Do you want this for yourself?) If not, look at how often you treat your co-workers or employees that way. The next time you are tempted to, try a little "Gold + Platinum" – and watch the results you get.

Here are a few ways you can apply it:

Communicate with your suppliers and staff the way you would with your customers. (Remember: Your staff treats your customers the way *they* are treated by you.)

How about having an employee AGM?
A newsletter for suppliers?
An "air miles" type of program for employees and suppliers who fly above and beyond the call of duty?

Be so bold as to ask people what would motivate them more. Invite them to design their own program. (It must be a win-win for them and the company.) And then implement it! See how it works. Refine and improve it.

Gold + Platinum = Rich Results

3. **Speak about your vision and passion.**

- *People are hungry . . .*
  . . . for something that moves them. Something they can buy into, and feel proud to be part of. Something that feels good and makes a difference.

  When you communicate your values and what moves you, people feel it. They are attracted by it. It will lead to more commitment and loyalty within your relationships or organization. (But remember: Do not seek loyalty unless you are prepared to give it back.)

  Express your vision and passion. But it is even more important to help people find their *own*. That is what they are really looking for.

4. **Take a risk in your communication.**

- *Listen to what people are saying.*

  A friend of mine attended the annual meeting of a major airline. It had been many years since the company had paid any dividends. Shareholders were upset. Some proposed that instead of profits, they would like to receive some perks, such as free flights. But the CEO refused, saying it was too expensive.

  What the CEO failed to do was hear the underlying message: People wanted *something*. It didn't have to be free flights. Shareholders did not want the company to be in the red, either. But something would be better than nothing.

  Are you ever faced with such a situation? Instead of seeing what is *not* possible, find something that is. Tell people you'd like to find it. Invite them to work with you to develop practical, win-win ideas. By hearing the real message, you will help build the spirit in your organization.

- *Don't play it too safe. Reveal yourself.*

  Some of the key messages in business these days sound like this: "Don't be vulnerable. Play it safe. Cover your rear end. Don't tell people what is happening. If times get rough, get the other guy before he gets you."

  To me, that is not the way to do business. It just does not compute. You get out what you put in. Is that what you want to get back? I think it is better to be honest with people. Even if you have to peel back your pride a little.

  Remember the third leadership step? *Take risks.* Say you were mixed up or made a mistake. Try telling people that you do not know what to do — and that you need their help.

  At the end of the day, the bottom line is more than money. It is peace of mind, fulfillment. If you are always covering your butt, you are not going to be happy. And *that* is *my* bottom line.

  "But won't I get fired?" It's possible. However, I think the people we work with want honesty more than they want perfection. We can deal with things that go wrong. Honesty salves the wound; lying burns a deeper hole within us.

> *INTEGRITY is everything.*
> *Without it, you go nowhere and lead no one.*
>   — DENNIS MCDERMOTT

When Peter Munk [chief executive of Toronto-based Horsham Corp.] apologized for his company's failure to enhance shareholder value, he set a rare example of executive candor.

"We have failed in the most fundamental responsibility that a public company has toward its shareholders and that's really the delivery of value to you," Munk told Horsham's annual meeting. "It's not acceptable, we shall not live with it, and we shall do something about it."

Munk heads a holding company with controlling interests in Barrick Gold Corp., developer Trizec Corp. Ltd., and oil refiner Clark USA Inc.

Excerpted from *The Toronto Star*, March 20, 1996

- *Tell people what you want.*

  I do a lot of marketing by mail. On one occasion, I drafted a promotional letter and sent it to my writing consultant for his comments. He said, "Peter, it's okay. But it doesn't tell people what you want them to do."

  That was a real oversight for me, because that's what I tell people to do in their speeches. For some reason I was nervous about doing it in a letter.

  Many people give information. Some say lots of "you shoulds." But few make clear requests.

  State what you want others to do. Clearly. Openly. Without fear. You could be surprised. They might do it.

- *Get help.*

  You have something to communicate. Do not waste your time. Get it out.

  Want to speak or write better? Find someone who already does. Someone whose work "sings" to you. Get them to give you some tips. If you need a speaking coach, find one. There are many excellent people out there. Want to communicate on paper? Get a writer. Find ways to put your best foot forward, instead of in your mouth.

- *Do it.*
  These days, everybody is responsible for the company's image. *You* are the business. Learn to communicate – and the company's success will be your own.

Communicators as Speakers

*To be more powerful,
use fewer words and more pauses.*
— Peter Urs Bender

"Communications" covers a vast terrain — from artistic performances to writing, from speech-making to the Internet, from poetry to music videos, and much more. There are so many different ways of communicating that it's impossible to address them all.

In this chapter, therefore, I am going to focus *mostly* on speaking and presenting. It is what I know best. For other modes of communication, I suggest you seek professional help; that is, find people who can help you in whatever area you want to learn more about.

What Makes a Good Speaker?

A good speaker has a number of these qualities:

- Intelligence, clarity, logic
- Enthusiasm, passion

- Values, humanity, compassion
- Humour, flow, fun, feeling
- Charisma, presence
- Ability to move the listener.

None of these guarantees greatness. The great shysters of the world used charisma. Many evil leaders have used passion. It is a package deal. The more you have in total, the more likely it is that you will be an effective communicator.

Who communicates well?

When I think of great speakers, I think of people like Winston Churchill, John F. Kennedy (and his brother Robert), and Helen Keller.

Certainly, the first three had strong voices and a forceful, precise, and stirring delivery. But the same was not true for Ms. Keller, who was blind and deaf at birth. She never became a "powerful" orator. So what makes the difference?

These people are memorable for two reasons: first, their messages were profound. And second, they managed to move their audiences to new ideas, feelings, and actions. You might say that the listener became more powerful, just by having listened.

WHAT MAKES A BAD SPEAKER?

Naturally, a lack of the qualities listed above will diminish a speaker's effectiveness. Here are some other barriers to good speaking.

- Failure to tune in to the audience's favourite: WII-FM ("What's In It For Me?")
- Tendency to see things only from one's own point of view
- Lack of honesty, and mixed messages (e.g., when words and body language say different things)
- Vague message that lacks specifics and does not give listeners

concrete actions to take
- Failure to connect with people, no eye contact, no emotion
- Lack of vision and risk-taking (a speaker who plays it safe).

Before working with someone, I try to remember
to ask myself, "What's in it for the other person?
How can I help the other person as well as myself?"
— JOHN ROBERT COLOMBO, AUTHOR

"Who Will Listen to Me?"

If you want to be better at what you do, there is one cardinal rule:

Practise, Practise, Practise

It's true for sports. It's true for professionals and doctors. (They have "practices," do they not?) It's true for writers, and for speakers.

"But who will listen to me?" you say to yourself. Start there. Start with *yourself.*

Are you aware of your "inner speaker," the self-talk that is going through your head almost every minute you are awake? Does it improve your confidence or put you down? Do you feel motivated by it – or do you resist the very thought of it? Listen to what is going on inside you!

Next, listen to yourself while speaking to others. How do you *really* feel about what you are saying? Are you being honest? Do you raise others or put them down? By listening to what you are saying, you are sure to improve as a speaker.

If you want more practice, there are many people out there who will want to hear you. Start by talking to friends. People at parties. Co-workers. Then contact local service clubs. Rotary, Lions, Kiwanis. They are often looking for speakers. Try the local business-improvement association. Business networks. From there, you can move on to the Board of Trade, the Chamber of Commerce, industry trade association meetings, and so on.

It is scary when you start. But remember: You do not have to be perfect. Your *goal* may be to become CEO or to be elected to public office. But you do not start there. So give yourself a break. Let yourself make mistakes and grow while you learn.

Speakers Also Need to Write

While I am a professional speaker, I also rely on the power of the written word to get my name in front of current and potential clients, the media, universities, and others who could be interested in my work.

One way I've done this is by submitting articles to local magazines, newspapers, and small trade journals. Publications where the style is not too formal and they are looking for contributors.

There are so many "niche" (or specialized) market publications, it would make your head spin. Magazines in real estate, boating, management, accounting, franchising – you name it. Not to mention trade association newsletters and in-house company newsletters. These provide an excellent way to get your ideas out and your name known.

Any time I have received an award, a write-up in the media, developed a new seminar, created a new book or audiotape, or have some news to tell, I also tell my prospects and clients in writing.

Here are some ways I have used written communications effectively:

Letters, brochures, promotional flyers, articles, books
- Content should be high quality and must be free of mistakes.
- Do them yourself if you are good at this, but use a professional editor. Also engage professional layout and graphic designers.

Press releases
- Should be professionally written. Crisp, clear, to the point. One page only.

Thank you letters
- Do them personally. Write them by hand. Mistakes are not desirable, but are excused.

Internet
- Do personal communications (e-mail, newsgroup exchanges, informal letters) by yourself. Mistakes are excused. Layout does not have to be fancy.
- Organizational and corporate home pages should be professionally done.

I consider life's two secrets to be
thank you notes and flowers.
— TOM PETERS

THE SECRETS OF SPEAKING EFFECTIVELY

How many times a week do you have to "present" yourself in person or over the phone? To customers or potential clients? At sales or departmental meetings? To your manager or boss, personnel placement consultants, or the bank manager?

Verbal communication has never been more important. Yet most of us are not taught how to present ourselves effectively.

A speech is *what* you say, the words you use to get your ideas across. A presentation is *how* you communicate.

In his book *Silent Messages*, Dr. Albert Mehrabian wrote that the believability of what we communicate (assuming the message *is* believable) is influenced:

7% by words, 38% by tone of voice, and 55% by body language.

Of this 55%, most is communicated by your head — specifically through your eyes, eyelids, eyebrows, and mouth.

Now, in addition to words, voice, and body language, think of the other parts of your presentation. Overheads, slides, and flip charts. How you handle the questions and answers. And all the other ways you connect and work with your audience.

Presenting is more than speech-making, and anyone can learn the skills to be a more effective presenter. In my book, *Secrets of Power Presentations*, I outline the five "quintessential" elements of a presentation:

1. Speech
2. Body language
3. Equipment
4. Environment
5. Preparation

All of these are important. Think of it this way. Would you have a "power presentation" if:

- You have nothing to say (speech)
- You look as if you don't care (body language)
- You want to show slides and your projector does not work (equipment)
- Your room is so hot that people are falling asleep (environment)
- You forgot to compose your speech (preparation)?

NOT LIKELY!

I am not going to describe these steps in detail here. That was done in my other book. However, let's take a little time to look at the content of your presentation.

A speech has three objectives:

- To inform
- To entertain and touch people's emotions
- To move your audience to action.

The length of your speech is not important. Getting the message across is. In general, the shorter the speech, the better. Most meetings are behind schedule anyway. Do not fill time – use it!

Inform your audience

It may seem overly simple, but the biggest problem for most people is knowing what they want to say. They have not taken the time to get clear with themselves and therefore they cannot be clear with others.

Before you make your next presentation, ask yourself these questions: What is the message *you* want to convey? Why are you talking to this audience? What are your objectives? Be specific in your answers.

Here is another exercise to help you.

You have one minute to tell someone *what* you have (your product/service/message) and *how* it will benefit them. What would you say?

List the major points on a piece of paper. Practise saying it in sixty seconds.

Try it a few more times. Then do it in thirty seconds. (But do not talk twice as fast! Leave out everything but the absolute essentials.)

This exercise will help you identify what is essential, and how to say it clearly and to the point. It is also good practice for when you are interviewed by the media.

You have now clarified what is important to you. Next, make your talk relevant to your audience. What's in it for them? Why will they want to listen to or buy from you? Remember to use language your listeners can relate to. Customers care about product/service features and benefits, price, quality, and value. Investors and bank managers care about profits and return on investments. Young people use words and concepts that seniors might not, and so on.

To ensure effectiveness and understanding, ask for feedback. Is the message you wanted to communicate the message people received? Were they inspired by your presentation? Interested? Bored? Watch their body language. Too many yawns, glazed eyes, and inattentive faces mean you are not connecting with your audience.

Entertain and touch people's emotions

This is one of the toughest things to do. I highly recommend that you do not tell jokes. What strikes one person as funny is often not to another. There is also the risk of offending someone, no matter how careful you are.

Start by smiling. It is the simplest, most powerful way you can communicate. If you are genuine, it conveys warmth, sincerity, and confidence.

Every so often (say every three to seven minutes), use some humour. I believe the best and safest way is to tell a story from your own experience. It could be about the problems you faced in starting your business, or different customers you have had. Share something stupid you did. (If you think you've never done anything stupid, ask your spouse.)

As you draw upon your experiences, your own emotions will surface naturally. If you convey them sincerely, your audience will feel the way you do. If you get choked up, so will they.

Begin on a light note. If you choose to get more serious and personal, do it when you and your listeners are warmed up.

End on a positive note. A good presentation should follow the MMFG-AM formula: "Make Me Feel Good About Myself." People need to be reassured that they are good human beings, and that they are in control of their lives and able to cope with life's challenges.

Sincerity is everything.
If you can fake that, you've got it made.

– GEORGE BURNS
(FAVOURITE SAYING OF DAVE BROADFOOT)

Move people to action

Generally speaking, you would not be making a presentation unless you wanted your audience to do something. Now is the time to "sell" – or make the case for what you want them to do.

If you have used the rest of the presentation wisely, you have already given them the facts. You've told them how your product, service, or ideas would benefit them. You've built trust and rapport. Thus action – or the "sale" – should be the next logical step for both of you.

In developing your talk, ask yourself: "What is the *one* thing I want people to do in response to my speech?"

Do you want your audience to buy your product/service?
Do you want your employees to adopt new behaviour?
Do you want these people to invest in your business?

Then say so.

As you do, listen to your voice tone and feeling. Do you feel afraid about asking people for what you want? Do you feel aggressive? Preachy? Desperate? Whatever your reaction, it is useful self-awareness. Your presentations will become more effective as you learn to be more direct and confident.

Give them more than just words

As I said earlier, you communicate more than words. You convey feeling. Enthusiasm and experience. And belief – the belief that you value what you have to sell or share. The more you develop these capacities within yourself, the more you can give them away to others.

It is also important to watch your body language. Are your gestures angry and threatening? Are you listless? Do you look as if you don't care about your subject or product? Put your soul into it. Be intimate, not intimidating. Show people the confidence that led you to get into this work in the first place.

I'd also suggest that you try to give your audience an *experience* of what you sell. Find a way for people to taste, smell, hear, and see it. Experience is far more powerful than words and lasts much longer. It also gives you an opportunity to have some fun by thinking up unusual ways to show your product/service.

If you sell pizzas, have someone deliver one just as you finish speaking – and give everybody a slice. Are you a banker? Give everyone a certificate for twenty dollars worth of banking services. (Would it be worth it to get a new account or a happier customer?) If you are a consultant, give away some valuable advice.

Demonstrate what you do. Show what you sell. Raffle a "free one" at the end of your talk. Find a way to give people a positive experience. Not only will you have fun, but others will, too — and they will remember you.

> *I hear — I forget.*
> *I see — I remember.*
> *I do — I understand.*
> — CONFUCIUS

TIPS TO BE A GREAT SPEAKER

- Smile. Take a deep breath. (It may be your last one — for a while.) Start speaking slowly.
- Never read your speech. Read your audience.
- Talk about your own experience.
- Compliment/praise others. It lifts you up when you give credit to others. Make sure it is honest and sincere.
- Communicate the basics. Talk about something you and your audience care about. Relate it to everyday examples. Don't be too academic, or you may lose your audience.
- Have some fun. Enjoy yourself. When you feel better, you communicate better.
- To be twice as powerful as you were before, say half as much and pause twice as much. It feels scary at first, but it works!
- Above all else: Be yourself.

> *Those who can express themselves well*
> *are steps ahead of those who cannot.*

WHAT BLOCKS COMMUNICATION?

Here are some things to watch for, and some ways to get around them.

Fear.
This is numero uno. The king of all blocks. It stops vision, wipes out passion, limits risk-taking, and blocks communication.

Fear takes many forms. It could be fear of what others will think. Fear of exposing your private self, your deeper feelings or vision. Fear of embarrassment.

How do you get past it? Start with acceptance.

It's natural to be nervous! Everyone is under stress when speaking in front of a group. (If you're not, maybe you should get help . . .) I give up to one hundred speeches a year and before each one, I am still nervous. But the audience doesn't see it.

Accept your fear. See the situation more clearly. Once you feel a little more at peace, get clear on your vision. Remember to breathe. Then give them everything you've got.

If we do not accept, we will never overcome.

Unclear objectives.
This is why self-knowledge is so important. Know what matters to you; how you think and feel. Communication will become easier.

Too little preparation = Too much pressure.
If you don't give yourself enough time to prepare, you are adding pressure – which creates *STRESS* – which in turn blocks your flow of ideas, words, and feelings. The purpose of preparation is to give you time to relax and get the flow going. To organize your ideas. To prepare any papers, handouts, audiovisual materials, exercises. To test your equipment. And to prepare yourself – mentally (clarity, concentration, knowledge) and physically (voice, breathing).

Always give yourself more time to prepare
than you think you will need.

Feelings.

Actually, it is what you do with your feelings that creates the problem. If you suppress, deny, or judge them, you will not be aware of how you really feel. You will not be able to draw on them when you speak. As a result, you will have less power and reduced ability to touch the audience's emotions. If you are angry or upset inside, it will show through your body language.

Try acknowledging how you feel. Ask yourself a simple question: "How am I feeling?" Be still for a moment. Breathe deeply. Let the energy that is blocked in you start to move. Even bad feelings will start feeling better if you let them flow.

A failure to be who you are.

If you are a selfish, ignorant, or arrogant individual in a one-to-one conversation – then you should be the same in front of a group. Please do not become *Mr.* or *Ms. Integrity*, pleading for teamwork! Be who you are.

Too much focus on yourself.

First connect with yourself. Then TFAY – *Totally Forget About Yourself.* Connect with your audience. Make eye contact. Watch body language. Sense the energy or feeling in the room. You will pick up important signals of what to say and do. If you are too focused on your own agenda, you will miss them.

> When I am giving a talk, I arrive well in advance. Always. I do not talk or answer questions. I give myself time to feel good. As I sit in the room, I connect with myself and the space, and watch the people. Then I ask myself: "What's in it for them?"

A resistance to learning communication skills.

Good communication takes more than talking. Think of the best speakers you have ever heard. Kennedy. Churchill. They were not great by accident. They worked at it.

Take Bill Gates as another example. Before the launch of Windows 95, he hired some of the United States' best consultants on public speaking. He learned how to communicate on camera and to improve his presentations in front of groups. The difference was like night and day. This enabled him to become an effective presenter for Microsoft, as well as its mastermind.

Most people do not know what really good communication is. Few of us have real-life role models for it. Therefore we do not value it. I suggest you listen to some top quality speakers. Experience what it is like to be really informed or moved. Then learn the "how-to" for yourself.

Communication in Your Organization

If communication in your organization is "fair" to downright "rotten," you are not alone.

As I said, most of us do not value good communication – because we don't experience it. We *are* used to experiences like being told what to do by our superiors; having communications breakdowns with our spouses, children, or parents; denying our own feelings and ideas. These are our models.

So what can you do? Start by identifying good communicators in your organization. Learn from them.

Speaking like a leader

Just imagine that you have to speak before a meeting where:

- Staff are upset about departmental practices or policies
- Management and employees fear for their jobs
- Board members are worried by low (or no) profits
- Shareholders are upset about low share prices or no dividends.

Would you want to present to a group like this? Maybe not. But you may *have* to! Here are some ways to leave a lasting, positive impression with your audience.

1. **Lead from within.**
   First, you have to come to terms with your company's (or department's) situation. Be it ever so difficult, the facts are the facts. If you are afraid – or at peace – with them, you will communicate those thoughts and emotions (in your words, voice, and body language).

2. **Find the real positives.**
   What gives you hope for the future? Communicate it! If it inspires you, it will inspire others.

3. **Deal with the negatives head-on.**
   Tell how you feel about where your department or company is going. If they know it concerns you – if they feel your feelings – they will be more understanding and less hostile. When people feel you are masking the truth (or lying outright), they really get upset.

4. **Listen to their input.**
   When people are disgruntled, they want someone to listen to them; to hear their pain and frustration. Instead of trying to tell them everything is rosy when you know it's not, just listen.

   Rather than reject "crazy" ideas, see if you can build on them. These may hold the seeds to the answers you are looking for to increase their satisfaction *and* your company's profits.

6. **Smile.**
   But make it genuine. Find something in all this to smile about. Remember that you – and your audience – are only human. The world is not going to end because of this (it just seems like it!). Be compassionate with yourself; don't beat yourself up. Also, be thankful for what you *have* been able to accomplish.

7. **Relax.**
   Breathe into your abdomen, and notice the feelings in your

body. This will begin to relax you. It will increase the amount of oxygen getting to your lungs and your head (so you will feel and think better). It will also improve your voice. You will sound more confident. (If you need more help, check your phone book under "Relaxation.")

8. **Present the facts.**
   Cleanly. Simply. Get help to prepare professional graphics/ slides or computerized visuals. Help people really see where the company is. They will leave feeling satisfied at having been told the truth – and you will be able to sleep at night.

9. **Find your passion – and share it.**
   Listeners want more than facts. They want to feel good. So give them your enthusiasm. Tell them why you believe in the organization. Where you want to go in the future. What you are prepared to do to get there – and what help you need from them to make it happen. (Remember: Everyone is responsible for where the company is, not just you.)

10. **Practise beforehand.**
    Know what you are going to say. Practise smiling, breathing, and speaking with power. Rehearse using your slides or computer so you know they work. If you are up to it, try it out on your family, friends, or a small group of staff or suppliers.

11. **Have some fun.**
    Sounds crazy. But if you choose to, your brain will find a way. Find some humour in the midst of this mess, and you will turn a near funeral into a resounding success.

Take the time to learn how to become a better speaker and communicator. You will enjoy it – and your company, association, country, spouse, and family will be glad you did.

Don't worry about the money. It will come.
Don't worry about the reputation. It will come.
Worry about the content of what you are presenting.
That is everything.
— DAVE BROADFOOT, COMEDIAN

Try altering your communications in day-to-day situations such as conversations, meetings, whatever. Speak more loudly, or softly. Express yourself passionately about something. Try listening more. When you feel uptight, breathe a few times and then speak. Smile. Remain silent if you usually speak up a lot. Watch how you feel and how others react.

If you are making presentations, learn the basic skills. Read *Secrets of Power Presentations* or any other good book on the subject. Teach others what you are learning. Discuss it and apply it. This is an excellent way to learn more quickly.

You can also build in opportunities for more communication. One of my clients, a Canadian electrical contractor, designed their office building with wide corridors to encourage people to stop and talk in the halls – a great way to build interaction and communication.

The next time you are in a meeting or talking with others, watch your communication and theirs: What is working? What is not working? What do you want to experience?

TAKING ACTION

REVIEW WHAT YOU'VE LEARNED . . .

Attitudes + Behaviour ➡ Results

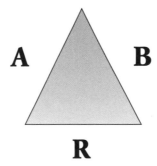

A **B**

R

Attitudes

- Communication is a connection between people. It is the exchange of information and feelings that leads to understanding.

- The better you know yourself, the better you will be at communicating your hope, fear, energy, enthusiasm, vision, and love.
- Everybody gets nervous speaking in front of a group. Accept your imperfections, then do it anyway.

Behaviour

- Communication is like leadership. There are practical skills you can learn to get better at it.
- Keep practising. Speak, write, and get your message out.
- Express what you feel deeply, and say what is on your mind. Honest expression refills the soul.
- You are continuously communicating how you think and feel through words, tone, and body language. (Watch what messages you are giving out!)

Results

- Some people will be eager to hear more. They will give you support and encouragement.
- Some people will not want to listen or hear more. They will pass you by.
- You will have the satisfaction of expressing yourself, touching some people's emotions, and moving them to action. (That is being a leader.)

. . . And Strengthen Your Leadership Muscles
(Exercises)

1. Ask

a) Ask for feedback on how you communicate and what you could improve. Try this in your job or association, with friends and family.

b) After a meeting, give and receive feedback. One way is to pass around feedback sheets. Title each page: "How could [Name of Person] be more effective in communicating?" Use one sheet per person. Each person in the room contributes an idea to every other person's page. (Note: Tell all participants to make the feedback helpful, and to remember that others will be giving them feedback too.)

c) Where does your communication with others continually break down? In the words? Emotions? Do you try to push your ideas onto others? Are you closed to the ideas or feelings of others?

d) At the next party you attend, watch yourself: How well do you listen?

2. Act

a) Set two communications-related goals this week: one personal; one business. (Remember: The goals should be SMART.)

b) Set yourself a penalty for not accomplishing your goals.

For your business goal: _____

For your personal goal: _____

c) Communicate more often. Speak up at a meeting. Write a letter to the editor. Write an article for a local newspaper or trade magazine. Talk with your co-workers about issues that are on your mind. Do it. Do it. Do it.

3. Associate

a) Find three individuals who communicate well in their speaking and presentations. (Or in written communications, if that is what you are more interested in.)

b) Watch them. Study them. Ask them how they do it. See if they have any of their own secrets.

c) Join an association, club, Toastmasters, or night school to learn more about communicating effectively.

I don't care how much you know. If you are
not able to explain it to me, you know nothing.
– DAVID CONRATH, DEAN, DEGROOTE SCHOOL OF BUSINESS

CHECK PROGRESS AND RESULTS

Measuring Progress and Understanding Success

You never get what you expect,
only what you inspect with respect.
— Favourite Saying of Roger E. Keeley, Past President,
Canadian Professional Sales Association

Leadership from within starts with these questions:

Where am I now (in terms of my life, career, fulfillment)?
Where do I want to be?

It becomes "real" by taking action – to move from where we are now to where we want to be.

But life is not fair, and we are not perfect. We don't reach our goals instantaneously. Success may take many weeks, months, or years to achieve, if it comes at all.

So how do you know if you are making progress? And how will you know when you achieve success?

It is great to have an idea.
But "the proof is in the pudding."

What Are Progress and Results?

Results are the outcomes of your attitudes and actions. The benefits of your efforts and the fruits of your labour. Results are life's way of giving feedback on how you are doing (now that you no longer have teachers and school report cards!).

Progress is the advancement you have made towards your goal. The change, or difference, between where you started and where you are at this moment.

Success is about reaching your destination – and enjoying the trip.

Each day, we grow and change in many ways. We get older. We provide more products and services. We meet new people. We earn more. We become fatter or thinner (you wish!). We learn more. Some of these changes are intentional. Many are not.

The purpose of a goal or objective is to make intentional progress towards something we value. We then use our attitudes and behaviour – our ideas, feelings, talents, skills, and tools – to try to create the results we want.

Why Are Progress and Results Important?

At the beginning of this book, I said that we are faced with many challenges. We need leadership to deal with those challenges and to make more progress in creating the results we seek.

In specific terms, the goal may be progress in business. Providing better service to your customers, staff, and suppliers. Increasing the quality of your products or services. Improving the financial well-being of your organization.

The goal may be progress in society. Helping those who have less (education, food, income) to have more. Improving the health of our communities, our environment, our economy. Exploring and understanding the earth, the stars, and ourselves.

The goal is also personal progress. Improving our own health and well-being. Being more creative and understanding. Managing the changes and pressures of life. Having more satisfying relationships.

These kinds of progress are all tied together. Our personal well-being affects how we feel at work. Conditions at work affect the quality of what we do and produce. What we create affects people throughout society, and how they feel affects us.

If leadership is about choosing – how we want to live and what we want to create – then results become our bottom line. They help us see if we are moving towards our goals, and whether our visions are becoming reality.

How Do We Measure Results?

We measure results in hundreds of ways every day. While making dinner. Travelling. Creating a new product. They are essential to making our lives work. Here's how.

We have an idea, a vision. We take action. Then we see what the results are. How does it taste? Are we there yet? Does it work? Do people like it? This feedback lets us know how we are doing.

In business, we measure or check things like:

- our income, expenses, profits, and return on investment
- our budgets; are our estimates on track?
- the number of products we have made or sold
- customer satisfaction; do they want changes?

It's important to measure both "hard" results (numbers, dollars) and "soft" results (company morale and spirit, customer satisfaction).

Assessing results is essential in all areas of life. To be healthy and successful, we need feedback from our:

- bodies – on our physical health
- feelings – about our mental/emotional fitness
- relationships – on how well we are communicating and treating each other
- organizations – on how they are running, and whether they are creating results and fulfillment

- nature – about whether it is clean and healthy, and whether our activities are sustainable.

The value of measurement

There are three benefits to measuring progress and results:

1. It shows us where we are now (versus where we were and where we want to be).
2. It tells us whether we are heading towards our goal(s).
3. It allows us to make improvements along the way.

Measurement makes us aware. It makes us focus on what we value and where we are going. It keeps us on track. And it gives us specific information about what is happening to us along the way. We can then use this information to continue what we are doing – or change it – depending on whether we are creating the results we wanted.

What we measure gets improved.
– PETER F. DRUCKER

So watch what you measure!

As you saw with the personality analysis, our greatest strengths can also become our greatest weaknesses. While "measurement" is an essential part of our scientific and economic way of life, it's not perfect!

Not everything that can be counted counts,
and not everything that counts can be counted.
– ALBERT EINSTEIN

Only certain things can be measured. For example, if we are looking at "success," many people will use "income" as the yardstick. Or "profit," for organizations. What about all the other factors that are part of success? Happiness. Friendships. Time to enjoy life. The quality of our air, rivers, and lakes.

These are all vital. But *because they are not measurable, they are often not valued*. That is a mistake.

To maximize progress – personally and collectively – we need an "integrated" bottom line. One that combines the well-being of all four major parts of our lives:

- economic
- environmental
- social
- personal/health

It is the health or well-being of all of these together that creates progress. For ourselves and for others.

Remember: If what we measure gets improved, it is *what* we measure that counts.

Measuring Well-Being

	Individual	Company	Societal
Economic	Income Savings	Income/sales Profit	Tax revenues Levels of employment
Environmental	Quality of air, drinking water Safety of parks, beaches	Pollution Access to resources	Safety/sustain- ability of environment Cost of cleanup
Social	Access to education, transit, housing	Availability of skilled people, reliable suppliers	Quality of schools Cost of social services
Personal/ Health	Wellness Relationships Security	Employee well-being, productivity	Community spirit Cost of illness Effects of violence

Circles of Progress*

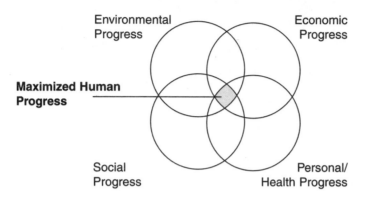

*Adapted from *Municipal State of the Environment Reporting in Canada* (Environment Canada, 1995)

We maximize human progress by maximizing progress in *all* the circles.

HOW DO WE MEASURE SUCCESS?

Success is hard to define. Some see it as achieving a goal. Others see it as enjoying the journey. The measuring stick depends on the result you seek. So what is it we are seeking?

In looking at that question, Dr. Deepak Chopra, former chief of staff at New England Memorial Hospital, says in his video, *The Way of the Wizard*, that humans have always sought "freedom." Freedom, he says, can be described on four levels:

1st level: The ability to "do what I want, when I want."

2nd level: The ability to fulfill our desires; material, emotional, mental, and spiritual.

3rd level: The ability to escape from our past conditioning (where we react to/are triggered by people and circumstances).

4th level: The ability to make spontaneously correct choices, spontaneous right action. Choices that lead to growth, evolution, and fulfillment for ourselves and others.

Chopra's levels are also a good way to describe the shift from the leader-from-without to the leader-from-within.

Success is very personal. It may mean money, power, or fame to some. To others, it is winning a competition. Helping underprivileged people to have food and a place to live. Creating a new way to cure cancer.

The idea of success takes us back to the first of the five steps to leadership: "Know yourself." It is only by knowing what is important to you that you will know if you have been successful in reaching it.

In our culture, many believe that success comes from having money and power. In my opinion, these are not sufficient.

I believe it comes from personal fulfillment. Feeling good about what one does. "Doing the right thing," as Peter Drucker put it. Being positive, creative, life-affirming. Adding to others' lives instead of taking away from them. These are some of the values that bring fulfillment; however, each of us needs to find our own.

It's one thing to succeed. It's another thing
to really be fulfilled. I think that if you have success
and you don't have fulfillment, you really have failure.
— TONY ROBBINS

THE IMPORTANCE OF A "GUIDANCE SYSTEM"

If you saw the movie *Apollo 13* or have seen the space shuttle on TV, you will remember NASA's Mission Control. Part of its responsibility is monitoring the "telemetry" – the data coming back from the spacecraft. NASA monitors everything from the astronauts' heart rates to the oxygen in the cabin, from the amount of fuel remaining and the firing time of the rockets to how far the spacecraft has yet to go.

In a business, you need similar types of information. Financial data. "Are we in the black? Will we make our goals with current resources?" Production data. "What did we produce in the last quarter? Did we deliver on time?" Sales, service, quality, and satisfaction data.

The same is true for any type of project, whether it is personal or professional. These numbers or facts are the "guidance system" that helps you or your organization accomplish its vision or mission.

Let's consider another example – an upcoming wedding. Here's the situation:

The happy couple wants "an event they will remember." There will be at least 150 guests. The bride and groom will each have three attendants, and there will be flower girls and ushers. They also want a five course meal, a humongous cake, a live band, and an elegant banquet hall, full of decorations and flowers.

They have quite a job ahead of them! Now what would you suggest to help them make their wedding a success? (Do not tell them to elope . . .)

First, you might suggest that they set a schedule. This would include dates for finalizing the mailing list, printing and mailing the invitations, and confirming attendance; renting the hall and arranging for the caterer and the florist; contacting attendants, choosing colours, and arranging for fittings.

Along with the schedule, it would be wise to have a "who will do what" list – for the groom, the bride, the parents-in-law, and so on. Since budgets are tight, they will have to watch their finances closely. To make sure it all gets done – on time and on budget – they will need to check their progress along the way. (Whew! Maybe it would be better to find a ladder . . .)

Will everything be ready on time? The "pudding" will be *The Day* itself.

A silly example? Perhaps, but many will go through it (at least once) in their lives. Moreover, this situation has all the elements of *leadership* in it: Knowing what one wants. Having a vision – and passion! Taking risks, communicating with others, and working towards a goal.

So how does checking progress help you achieve results in this situation?

1. *You know where you stand.* Rather than hoping things turn out right, you know what has been done and what has not. Is there enough time to do everything? How much will it all cost?

2. *It helps you keep commitments.* First, you have committed to your-self and your spouse-to-be — you both want a successful day. Second, you've made a commitment to over 150 people to "deliver" an event. They will be depending on you. Third, caterers, banquet staff, musicians, florists, and many others are now your partners in making it a success. If your plans change, all of these people could be affected.

3. *It could keep the stress down.* If you leave enough preparation time, you can avoid being totally frantic as you near the Big Day. Remember: This is supposed to be a joyous time. Not just that one day, but also the months leading up to it. Set yourself up to *win* and to have *fun* along the way.

4. *It gives you flexibility.* If something is not on schedule, or if problems arise, you will be able to make changes to prevent disaster.

5. *You will know how much it is costing.* By checking costs as you go, you will know if you are on budget. You can change from a humongous cake to a small cake; a live band to a disc jockey. (Or you will know that it is time to see the bank manager for a loan . . .)

For this or any other project, your goals and schedules must be realistic (i.e., doable . . . without killing yourself or someone else). They must have flexibility, in case of change. They should also be tailored to the needs of all parties involved, rather than forced upon them. This reduces pressure and stress, and increases motivation for everyone.

For the best results, keep everyone who has a stake in the project informed, involved, and happy. If you help them do their jobs well, they will help you realize your vision.

If you fail to plan, you plan to fail.
– FAVOURITE SAYING OF ALEX BAUMANN,
SWIMMER, OLYMPIC MEDAL WINNER

WHY CHECK YOUR PROGRESS AND RESULTS?

In summary, then, here are some of the resons why leaders must check their progress and results in whatever kind of venture they undertake.

1. **Awareness.** You know where you are and what is going on (rather than "flying blindly").

2. **Stay on target.** In moving towards a goal, you will need to make adjustments in direction, schedule, and activities. Awareness allows you to do this.

3. **Know how much further you have to go.** Are you on target? Will you finish on time and on budget? Do you have that option? Do you need more help or more resources? Do you have them?

4. **Alignment with others' needs.** Who is working with you? Who is depending on the outcome of your work? If you make changes, how will others be affected?

5. **Problem correction.** By checking progress, you will see when problems come up. You can revise schedules, workplans, or commitments, if you need to, to maximize everyone's satisfaction.

6. **Feedback to those involved.** If you need to be on target, so do others. Keep them aware of the project's status, changes, what you need from them, and so on.

7. **Accountability.** A very important part of leadership is doing what you say you will do. Final results are your evidence.

8. **Accomplishing the goal.** There are great benefits and satisfaction in accomplishing your goals. Enjoy them!

Progress Comes from Responsibility

A key factor in the success of high achievers is taking responsibility. But what does that mean?

To me, responsibility has several parts. First, it means accepting the facts as they are, and making the best of the situation, whatever it is. Second, it is accepting the power we have to create the conditions or results we choose. It is being the "cause" of what happens to us, rather than the effect.

Losers blame others for what happens to them. The government, the weather, the mortgage, the bills, the kids. The boss, the spouse, or the economy. They feel that someone or something else has the power to control their results.

High achievers choose a different perspective. By taking responsibility for the results they create, they create more results. It is not that they have no problems or barriers in their lives. Everyone does. But high achievers do not give their "power away to these barriers." They take control of their circumstances. They know that by altering what they do, they will change what they create.

> I believe that the past was perfect to bring you to where you are right now. The future will be determined by the choices you make now. When you take responsibility, set goals, and work with what you have, you will be more likely to succeed.

Responsibility means exercising your power to choose your *attitudes* and *behaviour*, which together will determine your *results*.

Waiting for the Perfect Ladder to Success?

Many people live their lives wishing they could do or have more, but not achieving it. Others achieve extraordinary results climbing the ladder of success — only to find out that the ladder was leaning against the wrong building. So are goals and results really that useful?

I do not know for sure. I can only comment on my own life, and those I have observed.

In my opinion, goals and achievement *are* an important part of life. I know my life has been richer because of them. I think it is better to climb any ladder – even if it's the wrong one – than not to climb at all. The key is to check your progress and results along the way. If you do, you will see when you are on the wrong ladder!

Remember that there are *two sides to results – inner and outer*. The inner results are the feelings and thoughts. The outer results are material things, conditions, and relationships.

To make real progress, you have to check *both*. It does not make sense to have all the money in the world and no personal enjoyment. Nor does it make sense to be frustrated because of a lack of money or success.

Don't wait for the perfect ladder on the perfect building. You will never find it. You will never make progress or create what you want in your life. Look for the ladder closest to you now and start to climb it. Check your results. Change ladders, or buildings, if you need to. The fact is, we all need to adjust things at some time or another.

There is no ladder to happiness. Happiness comes in climbing the ladder.

Getting there is half the fun.
– Author Unknown

An Integrated Approach to Creating Results

*Most decisions are
made on emotion,
but justified with logic.*
— PETER URS BENDER

The goal-setting, structure-and-schedule approach I have described is one way to achieve results. It works for many. But nothing in life works for all.

Artists and musicians create amazing results. So does nature, in all its endless beauty. Parents often do in the way they nurture us as children. We can experience great fulfillment on vacations and in close relationships. And we can create exceptional results in sports, hobbies, or helping others.

In all these activities, there is spontaneity. Love and caring. Wonder and expression. Freedom and exploration. These seem like the opposite of planning, measuring, and calculating, yet they still are essential to fulfillment. So how do we create the best results? Here's my observation.

The best artists have two things going for them: a knowledge of their craft, and the ability to express themselves creatively. Many artists see or hear their work inside before they begin to use their tools and technique to express it.

I think a "master" in any field must combine these two sides. You might call it the creative right brain and the logical left brain. The head and the heart. The craft and the art. Some Eastern cultures call it the "yin" and the "yang."

In a similar way, there must be two sides to our daily work. Inner and outer. Vision and action. Goals and soul-fulfilling, creative ways to reach them.

We need to integrate both parts to be whole, to feel fulfilled, and to be leaders who create effective results.

PEOPLE WHO CREATE EXTRAORDINARY RESULTS

Who do you think has created extraordinary results? Wayne Gretzky. Lee Iacocca. Bill Gates. Mother Teresa. How about Edison? Leonardo da Vinci?

There are countless people, past and present, who have done so. That is what has made them leaders. They are found in every field of human endeavour. Science, art, politics, business, religion. Service to humanity.

Who you see as achievers depends on what you value, on what matters to you. If it is money, you might think of someone like John Paul Getty or Aristotle Onassis. If it is political leadership, you might choose Abraham Lincoln or Winston Churchill. Science? Perhaps Galileo or Isaac Newton. Exploration? Columbus or Neil Armstrong.

What makes us remember these people? For one thing, we read about them in school and history texts. But it is more than that. These people *did* do something that stood out from the rest. They did it first, fastest, or farthest. Or perhaps their accomplishments changed our way of living, thinking, or seeing our world.

Remember what *you* have done

In thinking about extraordinary results, don't just focus on what famous people have done. Think about what *you* have accomplished that went beyond the ordinary. Maybe it was not as revolutionary as the accomplishments of Einstein or Michelangelo. But it is still important.

Maybe you reached a huge sales goal. Created a new product or service. Started a successful franchise. Pioneered a new system or program. Created a successful company. Served customers better than anyone else in your organization. Or maybe you made a big difference in someone's life.

Whatever it was, recapture the feelings. Replay the tapes. Remind yourself of the vision and passion you have had. You will have them again.

How to Improve Your Results

1. *Be clear on your goal/vision.*
   If your vision is not clear, you cannot measure your progress towards it. You need to know what results you want!

2. *Measure and check them.*
   How will you measure your success? What information will show you that you have reached your goal? Will you measure in terms of:

   • time ("I'll complete this by a certain date")
   • dollars (your desired income level)
   • employee well-being (80 percent of employees say they like coming to work here)
   • customer satisfaction (98 percent say they'd buy from you again), or
   • something else?

   These are called "indicators," or key signs of progress. Check your progress and results on a regular basis. Compare them with where you want to be.

3. *Use an integrated bottom line.*
   Be sure to measure all the key parts. Outer results (profits or widgets produced) and inner results (satisfaction or well-being).

Consider what is important for success and fulfillment. For example:

- physical, emotional, mental, spiritual outcomes
- economic, social, health, environmental outcomes
- impacts on spouse, family, employees, shareholders, community, environment.

4. *Learn from your results.*
Use them as feedback to show you if you are going in the right direction.

Don't just look at your own bottom line. Talk to all the people who are affected. Customers. Employees. Shareholders. The public. Ask what matters to them. Each has something valuable to contribute. By finding out how to serve them best, you will also improve your own results.

> *A good leader is best when people barely know he exists. . . .*
> *Of a good leader, who talks little, when his work is done, his aim*
> *fulfilled, they will say: "We did this ourselves."*
> — LAO TZU (CIRCA 600 B.C.)

Next, listen to your gut and intuition. Your feelings, energy, and motivation level. Your health and well-being are essential to your overall success. If what you are doing is not fulfilling (or is killing you!), you are off course. Get out of it. Find a better way.

Sometimes we get too focused in our thinking. When that happens, listen to your body. Exercise. Get up and move!

5. *Start now.*
Get started towards your goal. Don't wait until you have found the perfect solution, ladder, job, person. Start now.

6. *Be persistent.*
I know. I said this already. But the lack of persistence *is* one of

the greatest reasons for failure. Non-achievers do not take consistent action *long enough* to reach their goals.

7. *Let go of what is not working.*
This is almost as big a reason for failure as a lack of persistence. Many keep doing what they have been doing, thinking the results will change.

Persistence *is* important. But you need to recognize when it's time to change tack. How long have you been doing it? Are you learning much from it? Are you regularly modifying, adapting, trying new things? If not, you are in a rut. Get out of it. Try something different!

Remember what Kenny Rogers sang in "The Gambler": "Know when to hold 'em. Know when to fold 'em."

8. *Appreciate your progress.*
Remember where you started and see how far you have come. Often we forget this. We only see how far we have to go. But this step reminds you of your success to date. It brings the good feelings you can build on to complete your journey.

9. *Learn from the experts.*
There are many things you can learn from doing. But not everything!

Think of your computer. Maybe you taught yourself the basics, like how to do a letter, a flyer, or a spreadsheet. Great! But stop and think.

You are using software that hundreds of people have spent thousands of hours working on. There is genius built into it! Find out what it can really do! Get some training from an expert who knows how to use it. You will save a lot of time, countless headaches, and you will accomplish more.

The same is true for the other computer you have – *your brain*. You are an incredibly powerful person. You are capable of far more than you can imagine. Find out *how*. Read and talk to those who are masters at what they do. Learn what worked for them.

10. *Continuous improvement.*

> When a plane flies, it is off target 98 percent of the time!
> The pilot or autopilot keeps checking the progress, and
> altering the direction to stay on course.

> We are like airplanes. We are continuously "off course" in life.
> That's why it's so important to

> - know where you are going
> - watch where you are
> - keep correcting your attitudes and behaviour so you will
>   reach your destination.

> To be on target is more important than to be perfect.

One of the secrets to continuous improvement is incremental
change. Keep adapting, making small changes, and do it every day.

It works in education, exercise, cold calling, and in many
other activities. Don't try to do it all in one day. You cannot.
Grow little bit by little bit. It's less painful and brings great
results.

(You might also want to re-read the section on "The
Relationship Between Effort and Return" on page 29. It's important to remember that change takes time, and most success does
not come "all of a sudden.")

What Blocks Results?

Being afraid to dream.

Many of us are afraid to let ourselves imagine what we really want. "That
would be too scary, sinful, or selfish." "I can't really do that." Or we just
can't see ourselves having that good a life.

Others have experienced past failure and would rather not get their
hopes up, fearing it could happen again. It is less painful to accept the
status quo than to dream about possibilities.

If you are blocked by these fears, you will sabotage your results. Choose to believe that living a successful, happy life is possible – and that you can live some of your dreams.

> *Expect great things and great things will happen.*
> *Around here, we are realists –*
> *realists who expect a miracle every day.*
>
> – MARY KAY ASH

"It didn't work before."

Watch out for those who say that something is impossible, or that it won't work now because it did not work before. It seems logical, but it's not.

For generations, humanity has dreamed of flying like the birds. As I mentioned earlier, even Leonardo da Vinci, one of history's greatest inventors, tried to design an airplane – and failed. But mankind had to wait until 1903 for Orville and Wilbur Wright to lead the world into the age of flight.

If people say it cannot be done, just say to yourself that the right way has not yet been found – and keep on trying.

"Don't bother," they told the determined doctor. "We've tried it before. It doesn't work."

The doctor was Frederick Banting, and he was determined to prove his theory — that the hormone secreted by the pancreas could be extracted, synthesized, and used to reverse the debilitating effects of diabetes.

Dr. Banting had observed that every previous researcher had used an extract from a dead pancreas. Working with dogs, Dr. Banting and his fellow researcher, Charles Best, took their extracts from a living pancreas. And it worked.

Countless experiments over the next year eventually led to the mass production of human insulin for the treatment of diabetes. Since then, insulin has saved millions of lives.

Discomfort with looking at results.

Are you afraid to see mistakes? To feel failure? To be criticized? You are not alone! That's the way we are raised in this society. We value success, but not the path to success. "Failure" has much to teach us. When you meet it on the road, learn from it.

The goal was not a priority.
Sorry if I say that. But if you haven't reached your goal, you probably didn't give it primary importance.

Look at the priorities in your life. How do you know what they are? By looking at what you actually do. You go to work. Earn money. Watch TV, eat, sleep (and a few other activities . . .).

When something is a priority, you automatically get focused on it. You put other things aside. You make choices that keep you on track. Decisions that support you in reaching your goal. You take risks and overcome many obstacles. And you create results.

This is not like making New Year's resolutions. Or saying, "One day I'd like to . . ." This is about deciding that you will and then finding a way to do it.

Loss of focus.
There are many ways to get lost:

Your goal/vision is not clearly defined.
You have lost a sense of its importance.
You have too many "priorities."
You get lost in busy-ness, in activities that don't produce results.
Competition overrides results. Many get lost in fighting with others instead of creating the results they wanted. This happens a lot in politics and in business.

Check your progress and results frequently. They will show you where you are and what you have to do.

Seeing only problems and roadblocks.
Some people can see only what blocks them – problems such as a lack of money, time, training, or support. They can't yet see how these obstacles can be overcome.

Others do not have internal permission to pursue their goals. They were told by family, teachers, or friends: "You can't do that." "This is too sissy or too masculine." "That is not practical." "This is what you should do." And now they say it to themselves.

Instead of accepting these roadblocks, question them. See if there is a way to get around them.

> Become a hurdler. Don't focus on the hurdles.
> Focus on the goal. Then run, jump, and go for it!

Choosing someone else's goals (but not your own).

Inner happiness comes from doing things that make *you* feel good. Helping others. Making money. Raising a family. Being successful in business.

What was right for your parents may not be right for you. What is right for you may not be right for someone else. You need to find your own way. You have to build your own temple. Discover what makes you happy and fulfilled.

Reluctance to ask for help.

Maybe it's pride, embarrassment, or fear of rejection. For whatever reason, most of us don't ask for help. If you want to hold yourself back, this is a good way to do it.

Take another perspective. Is there a way you can ask without risking everything? Start with something small. Pick someone friendly and approachable. Encourage yourself. Try it. See how it feels. Then do it again until it holds no more fear.

Not keeping commitments.

How often do you keep your commitments? "This project will cost . . ." "I will finish this work by . . ." "I will be there at . . ."

If you keep them more often, you will create better results.

Pressure and stress.

We apply enormous pressure to ourselves and each other. We set unrealistic goals and commitments. We may promise that "the project will be done by Tuesday . . ." when there is no way it can be ready before Friday.

We unnecessarily set ourselves and others up to fail. Then we go through anger, angst, resentment, guilt.

If you want out of this rat race, start allowing more time. More space to move, to breathe, to make mistakes. Try it when you are setting deadlines for others, too.

Results in Your Organization

I said earlier that many people are afraid to look at their results. We are afraid of not getting what we want, being failures, and feeling guilty.

Therefore, the thought of receiving feedback and looking at our results in organizations can be very threatening. Other people will see our failures. We start to remember past experiences of poor performance evaluations, failed sales targets, going over budget, being criticized in front of others. Every negative and embarrassing thing we have ever done.

How do you feel about feedback? About looking at your results? How does your organization handle these? Your answers will likely be clues to the results you are creating.

Here are some of the different ways people and companies look at feedback:

- "We'd rather not know."
- "You still have a job, don't you?" (If I have not said anything, that must mean you are doing all right.)
- "There are no gold stars here. If I do something wrong, I get a kick in the pants."
- "We praise people because they work harder for us."
- "People need regular feedback. So does the company. We need to know what's happening."

I believe we all need feedback. Find a way you can communicate it without increasing fear and assigning blame. Look for individuals in your organization who may have a talent for this. Put them in charge of "company feedback." Learn from them. See what it's like to give, and what it's like to get.

If you want to improve, consider these questions:

"What would we learn from our employees if they could speak up and be heard?"

If you are open to it, give everyone a feedback sheet. Have staff fill them in anonymously. Collect them and see what they have to say.

"Why don't we like to hear feedback?"

"How can we look at feedback as information that will make us even better or more successful?"

"How can we reduce fear about receiving feedback?"

Find ways to look at progress and results without fear and guilt — so that people will be motivated to use the information next time to create better results.

TIPS FOR CHECKING RESULTS IN YOUR COMPANY OR DEPARTMENT
- Pick a specific project to review, or look at the overall results of the department or company.
- Find ways to reduce fear and increase trust. (One way could be to talk about your own resistance or uneasiness at looking at company results.)
- Present information without condemning anyone.
- Find those in your organization who are less judgemental. Have them present the information.
- Ask employees for help and ideas on how to improve. (This will also show trust and openness.)
- Have employees say what is good about the organization.
- Undergo this evaluation regularly (e.g., four times a year).

TAKING ACTION

REVIEW WHAT YOU'VE LEARNED . . .

Attitudes + Behaviour ➤ Results

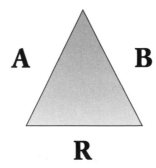

Attitudes
- To check your progress, compare it with where you started, and where you want to end up. To check your results, compare them with your vision.

- The purpose of checking is to see where you are, and to find ways to improve so you reach your desired result.
- Remember: "What we measure gets improved." Be sure to measure *all* of what is important to you.

Behaviour

- Define what is important. Use inner as well as outer indicators of success. Check/measure these as you work towards your goal.
- Use an "integrated bottom line."
- Keep your "partners" (clients, co-workers, suppliers) informed. If your being off target affects them, they need to know.

Results

- See the progress you are making. See what's working and what is not. Be flexible. Adapt and make changes. But do not stop until you reach your goals.
- Results are the fruits of your labour. The realization of your dreams. Achieve and value them.
- A leader is someone who creates results.

. . . And Strengthen Your Leadership Muscles
(Exercises)

1. Ask

a) Ask yourself: "Do I like the results I am getting?"

b) Ask others for feedback. "How could I be more effective?" "Are we getting the results we want?" Ask your family, friends, co-workers.

c) In what areas are you *not* measuring progress? Is this holding you back? Are you checking your financial results? Employee or customer satisfaction? Personal fulfillment . . . ?

d) Do you continually dream more than you create results? Why? What could you use in this chapter to help you make a move and create more results?

2. Act

    a) Start to check your progress in some area of your work. For example, look at how long it's taking you to complete a key project. Look at whether you are meeting your budget or sales goals.

    b) Build this into the new projects you start. Select key factors you want to measure. Check both inner and outer results.

3. Associate

    a) Look for three individuals who check progress, measure results, and use/communicate the information effectively, without guilt or blame. Ask them for their secrets.

Success is the progressive realization of a worthy goal.
— EARL NIGHTINGALE

AND IN CONCLUSION...

SOME PARTING WORDS

It's not what you know.
It's what you are doing
with what you know.
– PETER URS BENDER

At the beginning of this book I said:

1. **Leadership starts from within.**
   You possess the seeds of greatness in you, right now.
2. **There are skills you can learn to develop these seeds.**
   The degree to which you do so will determine your success.
3. **The biggest block to leadership is fear.**
   Let fear go. Be willing to stand out, to speak your mind and heart. Risk being criticized or looking foolish.

I will add one more right now:

4. **Believe in yourself.**
   Begin today to live the life you most want. Take that step you know you want to take, even if it is a small one. That is the way you begin the journey.
   Just do it!

Special Tips

*(Pssst . . . This idea will save your
company thousands of dollars . . .)*

Train Without a Trainer

"Sales are down. Problems are up. Pressure is building, and you can cut the tension with a knife." That's life.

So what can you do about it?

Some companies faced with this situation hire professional trainers or speakers to motivate and bring in fresh ideas and new skills. And to help the company boost sagging spirits, revenues, and profits.

Keynotes and seminars are very useful. Thousands of executives, managers, and companies will attest to that. As a professional speaker on leadership and presentations for over twenty years, I have seen how effective keynote speeches and seminars can be.

Yet there are several downsides. Professional speakers or consultants cost thousands of dollars. The time cost – for you, your managers, and staff to attend these meetings – is even higher; and as one-time events, their impact is short-lived.

So looking at it from your – my client's – perspective, I need to ask these questions: Is that money being spent as wisely as possible? How can you get the biggest bang for the training buck?

Here is my conclusion.

Many companies could be saving thousands of dollars annually by doing some of the training themselves.

That may sound strange coming from a professional coach. It seems a bit strange to say it. But it's true.

How to save big money

If your company is stagnant or failing, or you need a kick in the bottom line, don't start by spending thousands to hire an "expert." Try the twenty-dollar solution instead.

Use a book.

That's right. Use a book like this one, or one of the many other excellent books on leadership and management. (Go to a good business bookstore. Find one that speaks to you as you look at it on the shelf, or get a recommendation from a friend.)

Then read it. If *you* find it insightful or thought-provoking, buy a copy for every member of your staff.

Next, set up a weekly morning meeting, roughly an hour long. Start thirty minutes before the work day begins, and end thirty minutes into the day (so both the employee and the company have made an "investment"). Serve fresh croissants, good coffee, tea, and juice. Make the meeting informal and inviting.

Begin by sharing what you thought about the book and your vision for these meetings. Ask employees to read a chapter each week. Then discuss the book, in groups of eight or fewer, one chapter at a time.

You *will* get expert advice

Worried about using such a "simple" solution? Don't be.

There are many books on the market by highly qualified leadership coaches. Stephen Covey's *The Seven Habits of Highly Effective People* is just one example. By buying it, this one, or others, you are in fact consulting an "expert" to find out what to do. However, you will be using them the way they were meant to be used.

Hearing or seeing a good idea *once* is not enough. You and your staff need to remember it — and implement it — to turn your company around. That takes time and repetition.

This is the reason for holding your weekly croissant circles.

People first need to read the book themselves. To mull it over. Then in your meetings, they will get to hear what you and others think, to express themselves, and to say what mattered or made sense to them. That is where real learning, and change, begins.

Rather than telling people what to do, find out what ideas excite or speak to them. Ask them what *they* would do to improve the organization. If you find just one thing they *want* to do, it will have more long-term benefits than ten things they are told to do. Because the motivation, the spark, comes from inside. This is the fire you want to build.

More internal motivation will lead to less external motivation. That is, you will spend less time trying to create change, and more in enabling people to do work they care about — work that adds value to your organization. And their energy, drive, and focus will light the spark in others.

Not one session but *continuous* learning

Working with a powerful book will give you many months of payoffs. It may be tough to get rolling at first, but you will gather momentum over the four or five weeks it takes to read it. And the benefits will last beyond the last chapter.

You will be encouraging staff to share ideas and build positive relationships, rather than the kind they now develop in gossip circles. They will start having more fun at work.

You will be building in continuous learning. Your group will start looking for other ideas to act on, or bringing in other books to discuss.

They may even identify areas where they would like to learn more. At that stage you can bring in an expert to speak, train, or coach them in specific areas.

And there's more. Your staff will see you are serious about change, because you are involved, sharing yourself, and willing to listen to them and act on their ideas. They will also begin to see the power they have to affect the future of the organization.

With opportunities to develop their own ideas and solutions, guided by some of the world's greatest minds *and* your caring support, your people will find that leadership does not just come from head office. They will find that they have it *within themselves*.

FIVE STEPS TO PERSONAL AND PROFESSIONAL LEADERSHIP

PERSONAL

1. Know Yourself.
- Know your values – what is really important to you.
- Know your strengths/ weaknesses.
- Know where you need the help/skills of others – and find people with those talents.

2. Find Your Vision and Passion.
- See clearly what you want out of life – for yourself, your family, business, society.
- Think about possibilities and potential, not just what exists today.
- Whatever you do, do it with enthusiasm, joy, energy (if you do not have this, try doing it differently – or do something new).

CORPORATE/ORGANIZATIONAL

1. Know Your Company.
- Know what is going on in your company and industry.
- Know your company's strengths or niche.
- Know your people – not just the facts, but what matters to them "underneath."

2. Find Your Company's Vision and Passion.
- Know the company mission; own it; strive for it.
- Ensure your vision is compatible with your company's (if not, get out).
- Look within your organization – who inspires/motivates you?
- Find some passion for the company vision; share it with people around you.

PERSONAL	**CORPORATE/ORGANIZATIONAL**

3. Take Risks.
- Do daring things; take steps in unknown areas.
- Risk looking foolish and not being perfect all the time.
- Risk being vulnerable, forthright, emotional, human.
- Trust your gut/intuition.
- Make decisions and take action.

4. Communicate Effectively.
- Express your ideas and feelings; be willing to be seen and heard.
- You "stand alone" when you speak – learn presentation skills and develop confidence.
- Learn writing skills.
- Practise every chance you get.
- Communicate so your audience will understand and relate to what you say.

5. Check Your Progress and Results.
- Look at what is working and what is not.
- How do you feel about your life? This is a good sign of whether it is working or not.
- Look at your attitudes and behaviour; ask, "What is contributing to my progress; what is holding me back?"
- Make sure you have a goal or vision to focus your energy.

3. Take Risks.
- Tell the truth.
- Stick with your values, principles, and integrity.
- Be passionate, even when others are not.
- Take personal responsibility for the company's success.
- Make decisions and take action.

4. Communicate Effectively.
- Be direct. Tell it like it is.
- Share your vision of what is possible and how it can be done.
- Ensure people understand how to apply your ideas to make their own progress.
- Get feedback.
- Ask people what they feel and think.
- Raise people by praising them.

5. Check Your Company's Progress and Results.
- Look at what is working and what is not.
- If something is not working, take action to correct it.
- The more leadership you take, the more you will be given.
- Contribute to the progress of others – co-workers, customers, stakeholders; the more others benefit, the more you will.

Here are a few short summaries of key ideas from this book. Select the one(s) you like. Post them on your wall or bulletin board as a daily reminder.

WAYS TO BE A BETTER LEADER

1. Look at where you are now. Is it where you want to be?
2. Be aware of the results you want. Your vision or mission for living and working. What do you have a passion to do?
3. Take a risk. Make a choice or decision to act on that vision and passion. Select those attitudes and behaviours that will improve your chances of creating the experience you want.
4. Face what blocks or limits you. Do you not have enough money? Time? Skills? Will people think you are crazy if you think, act, and live that way? Is your idea realistic, doable? Are you afraid to go for what you want?
5. Express yourself, your vision, and what matters to you. Give feedback, input, suggestions. Listen to the valuable insights of others.
6. Look at your new results. How do you feel? Are you stronger? Happier? Better or worse off? What have you accomplished? What have you learned?
7. Get help. Learn from the masters. Learn from those who disagree. Learn what is working and what is not.
8. Do it again. See where you are now. Get clearer on what you want. Make new choices. Refine your attitudes and behaviour to get the results and satisfaction you want.

That is the essence of leadership: Choosing what matters to you. Learning how to accomplish it. Then doing it — to be more fulfilled and to help others.

Leaders . . .

- Demonstrate effectiveness
- Are personally disciplined
- Use time effectively
- Act with integrity; can be trusted; do not let you down
- Stand for what they believe, even if others do not agree
- See things from other points of view
- See end results, the final goal
- Have the ability to plan, step by step, to reach that goal
- Recognize and foster other people's talents
- Understand how people can work together effectively
- Are self-assured, not arrogant
- Know their industry (or subject) inside and out.

Daily Actions for Leadership

1. Write down your ideas, visions, dreams – keep a notebook.
2. Start with the result – see the completed vision in your mind and work backwards, to the present, to learn what steps you must take to get there.
3. Take action towards your goal/vision.
4. Learn something from everybody – every person, speech, book.
5. Learn the "how to" skills or the "secrets" of how things work – learn how others have been successful in creating results.
6. Exercise physically (it keeps the mind flexible, too).
7. Communicate yourself – keep your name and skills/ideas out in front of people (you do not have to be the best – just be "out there").
8. Find good people to help you, especially where you are weak.
9. Don't try to be perfect. Just do it.
10. Relax. Fear and stress block creativity and action.
11. Love what you do – and you will do what you love.

APPENDIX

Survey of Canadian Leaders

The following Canadian high achievers were surveyed to determine how they rated certain key ingredients for success. On page 35 you were invited to rate these ingredients yourself; now you may wish to compare their results to yours, by referring to the chart on pages 232 and 233. The ratings are on a scale of 1 (low) to 10 (high).

Eli Bay	Relaxation expert; President, The Relaxation Response Centre
Alex Baumann	Swimmer, gold medal winner, 1984 Olympics
Walter Bick	Founder, Bick's Pickles
Dave Broadfoot	Comedian; co-developed Royal Canadian Air Farce
David Chilton	Author, *The Wealthy Barber*; sold over one million copies in Canada
George A. Cohon	Senior Chairman, McDonald's Restaurants of Canada (and Russia)
John Robert Colombo	Author/editor of over one hundred books, including *The Canadian Global Almanac*
Mark Cullen	President, Weall & Cullen Garden Centres; broadcaster and author
Ken Danby	Painter; especially known for realistic sports figures
Dick Drew	Author, *Canadian Achievers*; nationally syndicated radio broadcaster
Arthur Erickson	Architect; designed buildings for Simon Fraser University

Ian Farquharson	Founder and Chairman, Speedware Corp. (software)
Sylvie Frechette	Synchronized swimmer, gold medal winner, 1992 Olympics
Jerry Goodis	Canadian marketing and advertising expert; author of *Goodis*
Hugh Heron	CEO, The Heron Group of Companies (home builders)
Peter Jensen	Sports psychologist; trainer for many Olympic athletes
Roger E. Keeley	Past President, Canadian Professional Sales Association
Theodore Kemper	Founder and President, Canadian Training and Development Group
W.P. Kinsella	Author
Laurier L. LaPierre	Author and television personality; co-hosted *This Hour Has Seven Days*
Mel Lastman	Mayor of North York, Ontario; founder of Bad Boy stores
Tom Leon	CEO, Leon's furniture stores; director of hospital foundations
Lewis MacKenzie	Major-General (retired), First UN Commander, Peacekeeping Forces, Sarajevo
Dennis McDermott	Labour leader; former president, Canadian Labour Congress
Don McQuaig	Co-founder and CEO, MICA Management Resources
Henry Mintzberg	Leading management expert
Raymond Moriyama	Architect; designed Ontario Science Centre
Betty Oliphant	Founder, National Ballet School of Canada
Peter Oliver	Founder, Oliver's Restaurants
Harry Rasky	Documentary filmmaker
Judy Rebick	Former head, National Action Committee on the Status of Women
Joerg Reichert	President and CEO, Mövenpick Restaurants of Switzerland
Seymour Schulich	Gold mining executive and investor; philanthropist (York University's Schulich School of Business)
Sam Sniderman	Founder and CEO, Sam the Record Man
Steven S. Staryk	Violinist; virtuoso performer and teacher
Larry Stevenson	Founder and President, Chapters Inc.

Don Tapscott	Influential media guru and author of *The Digital Economy*
Jerry White	Financial expert, author, and media personality
John Wildman	President, The Fitness Institute

Some of this biographical information was found in *The 1997 Canadian Global Almanac*

Leaders' Ratings of Ingredients for Success

Name	Good with People	Positive Attitude	Loving What You Do	Doing What You Love	Desire to Succeed	Belief in Yourself	General Knowledge	Knowledge of Your Field	Associate with Right People	Goal-Setting	Persistence	Hard Work	Checking Progress/Results	Communication Skills	Risk-Taking	Having Passion	Having Vision	Personal Values/Ethics
Baumann, Alex	9	6	9	10	10	10	5	9	6	9	10	10	8	8	7	9	10	10
Bay, Eli	9	10	8	9	9	10	8	8	7	6	10	8	6	8	7	9	10	8
Bick, Walter	10	10	10	10								10						10
Broadfoot, Dave	7	9	10	10	10	8	9	9	3	6	10	10	6	8	10	8	8	10
Chilton, David								10				10	4	10	5	10		10
Cohon, George A.	10	10	10	10	10	10	7	8	8	8	10	10	8	9	9	10	9	8
Colombo, John Robert	8	10	10	10	8	9	7	9	6	7	7	6	8	8	7	10	10	10
Cullen, Mark	8	10	9	9	8	8	4	10	10	6	7	9	8	7	7	10	8	10
Danby, Ken	9	10	10	10	10	10	8	10	8	9	10	10	8	10	9	10	10	10
Drew, Dick	10	10	10	10	9	10	8	8	8	10	10	7	8	8	8	8	8	10
Erickson, Arthur	5	9	9	8	6	9	8	10			9	9		6	8	10	10	10
Farquharson, Ian	8	8			5	5	5	5	8	5	7	10	8	8	10			10
Frechette, Sylvie	7	9	8	9	7	8	5	8		9	8	9			7	10	7	7
Goodis, Jerry	10	10	10	10	10	10	7	10	10	9	10	10	10	6	7	10	9	10
Heron, Hugh	10	10	10	10	5	10	5	7	7	7	10	10	5	10	10	10	5	10
Jersen, Peter	10	10	9	9	9	10	9	10	6	4	9	9	7	10	8	10	10	9
Keeley, Roger E.	9	10	8	8	8	8	8	8	7	8	9	9	7	10	7	9	7	8
Kemper, Theodore	9	8	9	10	10	7	9	9	4	9	10	10	10	9	9	8	5	9
Kinsella, W.P.	1	5	6	6	9	8	2	5			9	8	2	2	9	9	8	3

Attribute	LaPierre, Laurier L.	Lastman, Mel	Leon, Tom	MacKenzie, Lewis	McDermott, Dennis	McQuaig, Don	Mintzberg, Henry	Moriyama, Raymond	Oliphant, Betty	Oliver, Peter	Rasky, Harry	Rebick, Judy	Reichert, Joerg	Schulich, Seymour	Sniderman, Sam	Staryk, Steven S.	Stevenson, Larry	Tapscott, Don	White, Jerry	Wildman, John
Good with People	8	10	9	10	9	7		9	9	6	5	8	8	6	10	10	9	2	8	7
Positive Attitude	7	8	7	8	8	10	10		8	8	5	5	10	7	10	10	10	3	9	7
Loving What You Do	10	10	6	6	10	9	10	10	10	3	10	8	10	10	10	10	8	3	10	7
Doing What You Love	10	8	6	5	10	5	10	10	10	3	10	8	8	10	10	10	8	9	10	7
Desire to Succeed	6	10	9	8	10	8		8	8	8	4	10	8	10	10	8	7		10	10
Belief in Yourself	9	10	9	9	10	7		10	6	5	10	6	10	8	10	10	8	8	10	8
General Knowledge	8	8	8	9	8	2		9	7	3	8	5	8	8	5	10	6	8	8	6
Knowledge of Your Field	8	8	10	7	10	10	6		10	10	9	3	5	8	8	9	10	10	6	8
Associate with Right People	7	7	5	4	4	5		2	6	10	2	3	10	8	1	10	9	3	4	8
Goal-Setting	7	10	6	6	8	6		8	8	8	5	2	10	8	3	10	7	5	6	7
Persistence	7	10	7	7	8	10	10		6	10	10	5	10	8	10	10	10	8	9	9
Hard Work	8	10	9	6	7	9	10	10	10	7	10	6	10	8	10	10	7	8	6	10
Checking Progress/Results	5	10	4	6	5	5		3	9	10	5	4	10	8	1	10	5	3	4	7
Communication Skills	8	8	10	9	9	10	5	10	9	9	8	8	8	10	8	1	10	5	9	7
Risk-Taking	9	8	5	9	5	5	10	10	8	3	8	10	8	6	5	10	7	3	9	7
Having Passion	10	8	5	7	10	9	10	10	9	10	10	10	8	10	5	10	7	7	9	7
Having Vision	10	10	10	7	10	7	10	10	9	10	10	9	8	9	10	10	8	10	9	7
Personal Values/Ethics	8	10	8	10	10	8	10	10	9	7	10	6	10	7	10	10	10	10	4	6

The Personality Analysis

Here is an extra set of worksheets for the Personality Analysis (which was originally described in the chapter "Understanding Your Personality Type," beginning on page 59). Photocopy these pages before you fill them in again. This time, do one for your "home" personality. See how the score compares to your business personality. Have others fill them in — your spouse, co-workers, or staff.

Group

A Reserved, uncommunicative, cool, cautious, guarded, seems difficult to get to know, demanding of self, disciplined attitudes, formal speech, rational decision-making, strict, impersonal, businesslike, disciplined about time, uses facts, formal dress, measured actions. **Total score:** _____

B Take-charge attitude, directive, tends to use power, fast actions, risk-taker, competitive, aggressive, strong opinions, excitable, takes social initiative, makes statements, loud voice, quick pace, expressive voice, firm handshake, clear idea of needs, initiator. **Total score:** _____

C Communicative, open, warm, approachable, friendly, fluid attitudes, informal speech, undisciplined about time, easy-going with self, impulsive, informal dress, dramatic opinions, uses opinions, permissive, emotional decision-making, seems easy to get to know, personal. **Total score:** _____

D Slow pace, flat voice, soft-spoken, helper, unclear about what is needed, moderate opinions, calm, asks questions, tends to avoid use of power, indifferent handshake, deliberate actions, lets others take social initiative, risk-avoider, quiet, go-along attitude, supportive, cooperative. **Total score:** _____

Write your total scores below:

A = _____ C = _____

B = _____ D = _____

Next, determine which groups are larger and by how much:

A vs. C: Which is larger? _____
By how many points? _____

B vs. D: Which is larger? _____
By how many points? _____

Filling in the personality grid

Mark your results on the grid on the next page.

To determine where you fit on the vertical axis, look at your A vs. C result. For example:
If A was larger than C by 6 points, put a dot (•) at **A-6**.
If C was larger than A by 5 points, put a dot (•) at **C-5**.
If A and C are equal, put a dot (•) at "0," in the centre of the grid.

To find your place on the horizontal axis, use your B vs. D result.
If B was larger than D by 4 points, put a dot (•) at **B-4**.
If D was larger than B by 7 points, put a dot (•) at **D-7**.
If B and D are equal, put a dot (•) at "0," in the centre of the grid.

In the grid on the next page, place an X where lines extending from your two points meet. The quadrant you're in indicates your personality type.

Sample Grid

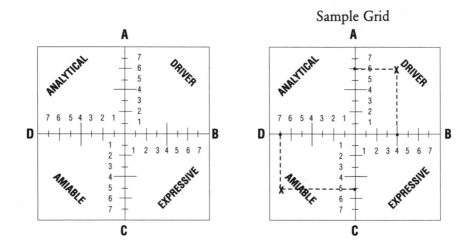

To interpret your results, see "Understanding the Personality Types," starting on page 63.

Index of Quotations

References

The following are full references to the publications and videos I've mentioned throughout the book. You may find some of them are useful companions to *Leadership from Within*.

Alessandra, Tony, and Michael J. O'Connor. *The Platinum Rule*. New York: Warner Books, Inc., 1996.

Bender, Peter Urs. *Secrets of Power Presentations*. Toronto: The Achievement Group, 1991.

Bolton, Robert, and Dorthy Bolton. *Social Style/Management Style*. New York: American Management Association, 1984.

Campbell, Monica, and Virginia W. Maclaren. *Municipal State of the Environment in Canada: Current Status and Future Needs*. Ottawa: Environment Canada, 1995.

Chopra, Deepak. *The Way of the Wizard* (video). Mystic Fire Video, New York, 1995.

Colombo, John Robert, ed. *The 1997 Canadian Global Almanac*. Toronto: Macmillan Canada, 1997.

Contemporary Authors, vol. 112. Detroit: Gale Research Co.

Covey, Stephen R. *The Seven Habits of Highly Effective People*. New York: Fireside, 1990.

Fritz, Robert. *The Path of Least Resistance*. New York: Ballantine Books, 1996.

Maltz, Maxwell. *PsychoCybernetics*. New York: Pocket Books, 1990.

Mehrabian, Albert. *Silent Messages*. Belmont, CA: Wadsworth Publishing Company, 1981.

Merrill, David W., and Roger H. Reid. *Personal Styles and Effective Performance*. Radnor, PA: Chilton Book Company, 1981.

Miller, Diane Disney. *The Story of Walt Disney*. New York: Henry Holt & Company, 1956.

1995 Current Biography Yearbook. New York: The H.W. Wilson Company.

Robbins, Anthony. *Personal Power II: The Driving Force* (video). Guthy-Renker Corp., 1996. In Canada contact Northern Response Ltd., Toronto.

Thomas, Bob. *Walt Disney: An American Original*. New York: Simon & Schuster, 1976.

PRESENTATIONS AND PRODUCTS BY PETER URS BENDER

Mr. Bender offers lively keynotes and in-house seminars on:

Leadership from Within
Power Presentations
Sell Yourself to Yourself

Books and Tapes

Special quantity discounts are available on:

Leadership from Within
Secrets of Power Presentations

Secrets of Power Presentations
Audio-cassette Self-study Course
4 tapes – 8 sides
with a 56-page workbook

Videotape Programs Also Available

Contact

The Achievement Group
108 – 150 Palmdale Drive
Toronto, ON Canada M1T 3M7
Tel: (416) 491-6690 Fax: (416) 490-0375

For single orders of books and tapes
call 1-800-668-9372